St. John Chrysostom
Old Testament Homilies

St. John Chrysostom

Old Testament Homilies

Volume One

Homilies on Hannah, David and Saul

Translated with
an Introduction
by
Robert Charles Hill

HOLY CROSS ORTHODOX PRESS
Brookline, Massachusetts

On the cover: Michelangelo Buonarroti, *The prophet Joel* (detail), Fresco, 1509, Cappella Sistina, VC.

LIBRARY OF CONGRESS CATALOGING–IN–PUBLICATION DATA

John Chrysostom, Saint, d. 407.
    [Homilies. English. Selections]
    St. John Chrysostom Old Testament Homilies /
    translated with an introduction by Robert Charles Hill.
        p. cm.
Includes bibliographical references and indexes.
    ISBN 1-885652-65-8 (v. 1 : alk. paper) — ISBN 1-885652-66-6
(v. 2 : alk. paper) — ISBN 1-885652-67-4 (v. 3 : alk. paper)
    1. Bible. O.T. — Sermons. 2. Sermons, Greek—Translations
into English. I. Hill, Robert C. (Robert Charles), 1931- . II. Title.
    BR65.C43E5 2003
    252'.014—dc22
                                        2003003988

To His Eminence Edward Bede Cardinal Clancy, AC,
in gratitude
for his ministry as archbishop of
the church of Sydney 1983-2001

Of this gospel I have become a minister
according to the gift of God's grace
that was given me by the working of his power.
Ephesians 3.7

Contents

INTRODUCTION

The reputation of John of Antioch as preacher and biblical commentator, winning him in later times the sobriquet Golden-mouth, rests particularly on his occasional sermons and his commentaries on the New Testament. It was his Commentary on the Gospel of Matthew for which in medieval times, we are told, Thomas Aquinas was prepared to give "the whole town of Paris," while no doubt it was Antiochene accents in his treatment of Pauline theology that prompted Martin Luther to declare him, by contrast, "only a foolish babbler."

Liturgical usage, if nothing else, however, obliged Chrysostom in his preaching ministry in both Antioch and Constantinople to comment on Old Testament works as well, both whole books and also excerpts appearing as texts for reading in the day's liturgy of his church (such as those from Isaiah and Jeremiah, as well as individual psalms, on which we have commentaries occurring in a later volume in this series). While his equipment for commentary on this material (exegesis in the strict sense being beyond him and his contemporaries) was more limited, he had no qualms in principle about breaking the bread of the Word from Jewish authors to his congregations, as his two homilies on the relative obscurity of the Old Testament (also included in this series) declare. And his lengthy collections of homilies on the book of Genesis (traditional Lenten fare in his church) and the Psalms (an early work, also by tradition) betray a relish for mediating Moses and David to his listeners only

1

less than his affinity with Paul and the evangelists.

These longer collections of Chrysostom's homilies on Old Testament books have already appeared in English and other modern languages. Hitherto untranslated, however, and therefore less familiar to modern readers are a score of homilies on biblical figures and prophets as well as several psalms and a treatment of Old Testament composition generally, which now appear in English translation from Greek for the first time. They shed further light on this preacher's approach to the Hebrew Scriptures in his local form of the Septuagint version, his abilities as a commentator, his style of hermeneutics and capacity for moral admonition and spiritual direction of his congregations. They also illuminate historical events in Antioch at the time, as uniquely they focus on figures from biblical history.

In his works generally, Chrysostom does not choose a character from the Old Testament historical books (or Former Prophets, in the terminology of the Hebrew Bible) for extended individual commentary. So when we find two series of homilies which – at least in the headings now assigned them – bear the names of David and Saul, in one case, and Hannah, the mother of Samuel, in the other, we have to wonder if this preacher and his Antiochene congregation – not known for particular interest in or sympathy with Jewish history or customs – experienced a change of heart. Our reading of them soon betrays the fact that both series show the preacher responding to sensational events in the life of the city of Antioch in 387, the year in which it came near to bringing down upon itself the savage wrath of the emperor Theodosius in Constantinople in the wake of vandalism perpetrated against the images of the imperial family on February 25. In preparation for (the eight-week) Lent, due to begin on March 1, Chrysostom was already engaged in a series of homilies (as usual, on Genesis), which took a sudden turn with the awful crime and its likely vindictive aftermath, and which have thus become celebrated as the Homilies on the Statues. While these have attracted much attention, as they also won the preacher much acclaim at the time, the shorter series on David and Saul, delivered (it seems) before the Statues homilies were concluded with the return of Bishop Flavian from successful intercession at the court, has been ignored. Although throwing light on the sensational events, they rate no mention from the modern editor of the Statues homilies, Franz van de Paverd, who also thinks the Hannah homilies of little relevance, though these latter were composed around Pentecost that year and show the preacher naturally still affected by the crisis.

We need to redress that neglect and study these two series of homilies, on David and Saul and on Hannah, not only for the light they throw on the historical events of 387 in Antioch, but also for an insight into Chrysostom's approach to the text of the Former Prophets, his skill as a homilist, and his role as pastor and spiritual guide. They appear in English translation from the Greek for the first time in this volume.

HOMILIES ON DAVID AND SAUL

The casual reader of these three homilies, unaware of their
historical context, to which the preacher does not directly
allude, would presume he has chosen for delivery to an
unspecified congregation some largely moral lessons on
human relationships based on incidents in David's life when
he had fallen into disfavor with King Saul. [1] The particular
lessons include forbearance under unwarranted provocation
and the sparing of wrongdoers' lives, amply illustrated by
David's refusal to take advantage of opportunities to even
the scores with Saul, despite the latter's wrongful grudge
against him and his own men's urging. The parts of the
Former Prophets bearing on these incidents include
particularly chapters 18, 24, and 26 of 1 Samuel; there is also
incidental reference in the homilies to the parable of (the
Unmerciful Servant and) the Merciful Master, Matthew 18.23-
35, on which "the other day," πρῴην, the preacher had more
fully commented, and which is clearly related in theme.

The content at first glance seems predictable enough,
susceptible of the moral emphasis for which this preacher,
like many another, has a name. We could ourselves almost
forecast the principal points which in our reading we find
inter alia emerging from the parenesis in the course of the
three homilies:

1. David has been wronged, and normally retribution
would apply.

2. He is under pressure from his men to seize the opportunity to take Saul's life.

3. He has been slandered by others, despite his many val-
orous deeds.

5

4. David does not choose to exploit the opportunity to slay Saul.

5. He can leave Saul to God.

6. Despite his sparing Saul, he still takes the initiative to address him deferentially.

There is little contemporary relevance, it would seem, in this commentary on the text.

As often happens, however, placement of these homilies in their historical context alerts us to a subtext underlying these innocuous platitudes, accounting also for the way the accent falls as it does. The vital clue comes in the reference to his commentary "the other day" on the Matthean parable of the Merciful Master, this commentary occurring in the penultimate homily of the series on the Statues about a week before Bishop Flavian's return from his visit to Constantinople to beg the emperor's pardon. The David and Saul conflict, then, the injured sufferer sparing wrongdoer in the Old Testament text (or creditor forgiving debtor in the Gospel parable), takes on a whole new meaning – never formulated but at every stage implied for the attention of David-Theodosius and his court. The subtext to the above points thus emerges:

1. The emperor has been insulted, and Antioch can expect punishment.

2. Advisers recommend severity on the offending city.

3. Bad reports about Antioch have reached the court, despite its good record.

4. There are practical advantages to being conciliatory.

5. There is a higher court that will judge and punish.

6. The emperor should make the first move.

It would seem, then, that far from this being an incidental series of homilies offering anodyne truisms to some uninterested congregation, we are reading a vital contribution to the reconciliation process between an offended monarch and a guilty city in danger of severe sanctions. Every listener in Antioch, and by text or word of mouth at the court, would be alive to the message of clemency being urged by the portrait of David in the homilies, this time presented as a model of gentleness, πραότης. No wonder we find the preacher's mood not as ebullient as usual nor his style expansive or florid; the tension is palpable, for the good reason that the bishop has still to receive and convey the good news of the emperor's positive response to the appeal, when Chrysostom will give vent to the public exultation in the last of the Statues homilies on Easter Day. (The Hannah homilies follow at the end of the Easter season, when the tension has lessened, though the incident is still fresh in people's minds.)

What we get, then, in the homilies on David and Saul is more than detached commentary on some passages from the text of the Former Prophets (read, of course, in his local Antiochene, or "Lucianic," form of the Septuagint), though the apt choice of the chapters from 1 Sam makes eisegesis unnecessary; no one present could fail to grasp their relevance. It is no surprise, then, that having achieved his ulterior purpose in selecting his text, Chrysostom can show less observance than usual of Antioch's characteristic attention to textual detail in fidelity to the principle of ἀκρί βεια, precision. He is even prepared at times to give the text a twist that respects his own purpose, not so much that of the biblical author. David's lament in 2 Sam 1 is presented in the second homily as noble grief at the death in battle of his old foe Saul, whereas the text indicates it was prompted rather by his friend Jonathan's dying with him. David's adoption of Mephibosheth in 2 Sam 9 is likewise presented in the third homily as a gracious favor to Saul's offspring, whereas in fact he is Jonathan's son, one moreover who becomes a traitor – a distasteful fact suppressed by Chrysostom as being irrelevant to the current situation and unlikely to impress an emperor under pressure to forgive and forget; ἀκρίβεια has its limits when a case is to be made.

Modern critical readers of the Former Prophets may feel the homilist has not always appreciated the dogmatic concerns of the author, anxious to trace the word of the Lord taking effect in sacred history. Chrysostom for his purposes, by contrast, wants to highlight moral issues, such as gentleness and forbearance; and he closes his first homily by urging his listeners (male only, it seems) to take up the sacred books at home with their wives and children (the domestic church, no less), and apply the examples found therein to their own lives. "In fact, if you want to talk about a king, see, there is a king there; if about soldiers, about a household, about political affairs, you will find a great abundance of these things in the Scriptures." In short, for them – as for him – the Bible is principally a moral and hagiographical treasury.

Relatively brief though the parenesis is in these homilies, with the homilist eyeing a different audience at the court, he claims to have reduced the congregation to tears at the close of the second homily. Those who missed that homily because of attendance at the theatre and its dissolute goings-on he berates in withering satire in one of his most stunning pieces of rhetoric at the beginning of the third: how could they dare "to listen with the same ears to shameful depravity and to Old and New Testament readings schooling you in the sacraments, μυσταγωγοῦντος?" For the guilty the only recourse is the ritual of public penance, "abasement," ἐξομολό γησις, practised by his church in the absence of a rite of private reconciliation; only then may they enter and "attend to the divine sayings." Admonition of his congregation, however, is not Chrysostom's principal concern in these homilies; and we gain less from him on the principles of Antiochene spirituality here than from a longer work with no hidden agenda, like his Commentary on the Psalms, or even the incidental homilies on the prophets, such as those in the next volume in this series.

The particular value of these three homilies on David and

Saul is the illustration they provide of a homilist finding himself at a critical moment in the history of his city of Antioch in 387, and interrupting a Lenten program to choose figures from sacred history enacting a drama also being played out at another level in the experience of his congregation. As such, they now make for riveting reading.

Homily One

*On the story of David and Saul,
On forbearance, the need to spare enemies
and not speak badly of the absent.*

When some dire and longstanding inflammation affects the body and proves hard to budge, there is need of a lot of time and effort, on the one hand, and on the other great skill in applying remedies if its roots are to be safely dislodged.[1] You can see this in the case of the soul as well: when you want to root out a passion that has for a long time been deeply rooted and is settled in, one or two days' exhortation does not suffice for its correction. Instead, there is often need of discourse on this theme even on many days if, that is, we are bent, not on display and titillation, but on benefit and welfare.

For this very reason, as we did in connection with the oaths,[2] speaking to you many days in succession (677) on the same theme, let us do so in connection with resentment as well, giving continuous advice on it according to our ability. This, in fact, strikes me as the best manner of instruction, not giving up advising on any subject at all until we see the advice reaching its goal. I mean, the one who discourses today on almsgiving, tomorrow on prayer, the next day on clemency, then on humility, will succeed in getting none of them right with the listeners by shifting from one to another, and then from there to something else without stopping. Rather, the person intending to bring to fulfilment in the listeners what he says must not stop exhorting and advising on the same matters nor move on to something else before seeing the previous recommendation firmly rooted in them.

This is what teachers do, too: they do not lead the children on to the syllables until they see the knowledge of the letters correctly learnt by them. The other day, then, we read to you the parable of the hundred denarii and the ten thousand talents, and brought out how vicious is remembrance of wrongs.[3] The man who was not brought down by the ten thousand talents, remember, a hundred denarii overwhelmed, canceled the pardon that had been granted, stripped him of the gift, landed him in court again after his being freed of liability, from there cast him into prison, and so handed him over to undying punishment. Today, however, we shall lead the address on to a different theme; there was need, to be fair, for the one speaking on both clemency and gentleness to provide personal examples of these excellent values so as to teach in word and instruct in deed. But since we ourselves are far short of this virtue,[4] let us cite one of the saints, and before your very eyes we shall produce a palpable and effective exhortation for you, like a kind of archetypal image, proposing the righteous man's virtue for your imitation and our own.

So whom should we cite in discoursing on clemency? Who else than the one receiving testimony from on high and especially remarkable in this case?[5] "I found in David, son of Jesse," Scripture says, remember, "a man after my own heart."[6] Now, when God gives his opinion, there are no grounds left for opposition: that verdict is proof against corruption, God judging not from favor or from hatred but making his decision on the mere virtue of the soul. It is not for this reason alone, however, that we cite him, that he received the verdict from God, but also because he is one of those nourished on the Old dispensation. You see, while there is nothing remarkable for anyone in the age of grace to be found free of resentment, forgiving enemies their sins and sparing abusers – that is, after the death of Christ, after such wonderful forgiveness of sins, after the directives redolent of sound values – in the Old dispensation, by contrast, when the Law permitted an eye to be plucked out for an eye, a tooth for a tooth, and vengeance to be taken on the wrongdoer in equal terms,[7] who amongst the listeners is not struck by someone found to surpass (678) the norm of the commandments and attain to New Testament values? is there anyone of those failing to imitate him whom he would not show devoid of both pardon and excuse?

Now, for us to gain a more precise knowledge of his virtue, allow me to repeat the words spoken somewhat earlier and mention the kindnesses this blessed man showed Saul.[8] I mean, there is nothing remarkable in not taking vengeance on an enemy who had simply done you wrong; but to be in a position to do away with this person when he had fallen into his hands, on whom many great kindnesses were conferred and who had endeavored to do away with his benefactor on many an occasion in response to those great benefactions, and to forgive him and snatch him from the schemes of others, though he was likely to set his mind to the same things again – what degree of sound values did he fail to achieve?

So let me briefly describe the favors David conferred on Saul, and when and how. The Jews were involved in a harsh conflict at one time, remember, all were cowering and terrified, none presuming to lift their head, and instead the whole city was at its last gasp, everyone looking death in the face, the whole people daily expecting to die, living a life more wretched than people thrown into a pit. This man emerged from the sheep to enter the battle line, and despite his age and inexperience in military endeavors he achieved deeds surpassing all expectation. Even if he had achieved nothing, he would have deserved the crown for enthusiasm and initiative alone. After all, there would have been nothing remarkable in some soldier of mature age doing this, the law of military service requiring it. But in the case of this man, far from his seeing some obligation lying upon him, he had many to discourage him: his brother upbraided him, and the king had regard for his green years and the extremity of the risks, held him back and bade him stay put in the words, "You cannot go because you are a stripling, whereas he has been a man of war from his youth."[9]

Despite his having no reason to prompt him, however, on his own account he was stirred up by divine zeal and love of country, regarded men as sheep and was bent on driving off this mighty army like dogs. So without qualms he made for the savages, and gave evidence of such great care for the king on that occasion as to set him on his feet after his lying on his face before the battle and the victory. That is to say, he not only was of help to him in deeds afterwards, but even beforehand he urged him in word and convinced him to take heart and have firm hope for what lay ahead, speaking in this way, "Let not my lord's heart fail, because your servant will go and fight with this foreigner."[10] Is this of little significance, tell me, for someone under no obligation (679) to give his life, and for the benefit of others to make for the enemies' ranks without sustaining any injury from them? Was it not necessary that an inscription to him as lord be made after this and for him to be hailed as savior of the whole city for preserving the fabric of the kingdom, the foundation of the city and everyone's life in the wake of God's grace? After all, what else could be a greater service than this? I mean, the favor he bestowed was not of money, not of glory and influence, but his own life itself, and he pulled him back from the very gates of death, and at least from a human point of view it was thanks to him that the king lived from then on and enjoyed his rule.

So how did he reward him in consequence of this? I mean,

were you to assess the very magnitude of the achievement, he would not have exceeded its merit if he had taken the crown from his head and put it on David's; rather, he would have been further in his debt. After all, the boy made him a gift of both life and kingship, whereas the king was destined to yield to him only kingship. In any case, let us see his reward. What was it, in fact? From then on he was jealous of him, and from that day forward he held him in suspicion. Why on earth, for what reason? I must tell you the reason for the jealousy. There is in fact nothing worth mentioning: what grounds for legitimate jealousy could there be towards the one who made you the gift of your life and gave you existence? Still, let us see as well the reason for the enmity so that you may learn that it was nothing less than the victory itself, and that he deserved to be honored for reasons that later formed the basis for jealousy and subterfuge.

So what did lie at the basis of the jealousy? When he took the savage's head and came back carrying the spoils, "the women came out dancing, singing and saying, 'Saul smote them in his thousands, and David in his tens of thousands.' Saul got angry, and was jealous of David from that day forth." [11] Why, tell me, was that? Especially as, after all, there was no need for him to be hostile to him, even if these things had been said unfairly; on the contrary, since he had come to know from experience his good will and the fact that without pressure or force from anyone he had put himself at such great risk from his own good will, there was no need to suspect any evil from him in future. As it was, however, the compliments were actually fair; and if there is anything deserving of comment, those who made them were more generous to Saul than to David: he should have been grateful for their conceding him at least his thousands. So why did it irk him that they granted the other man his ten thousands? I mean, had he been conducting the campaign and made at least some slight contribution, then it would have been appropriate to say "Saul in his thousands and David in his ten thousands." But if he stayed at home in fear and trembling, daily expecting to die, while the latter did it all, would it not have been absurd for the one who had no part in facing those dangers to be irked for not receiving more of the compliments? In fact, if any one was to be irked, it should have been David for personally carrying the whole thing off and having someone else share in the compliments.

Still, I raise none of these matters with you. [12] What I would like to say, however, is this: even supposing that the women were in the wrong, and (680) deserved blame and criticism, what did this have to do with David? I mean, he was not the one who composed the song, nor the one who convinced them to say what they said, nor was he responsible for this style of compliment. And so if Saul felt the need to be irked, he should have been irked with them, not with the common benefactor of the city, who was also deserving of ten thousand crowns. But them he forgave, and took it out on him. If the blessed man had been carried away with that eulogy, and had become envious of the ruler, abusive towards him and contemptuous of his kingship, the envy would perhaps have had some basis; but if he proved more equable and more gentle, and if he continued to adhere to the position of a subject, what reasonable grounds were there for his irritation? I mean, if someone accorded honors were to be carried away by it and become hostile to the one whose reputation he has eclipsed and insist on exploiting the honors to insult him, the ill-feeling would have some excuse; but when he continues to show regard, and is actually more attentive and yields pride of place in everything, what basis does the malice then have?

And so, had he rendered him no other service, he should have loved him all the more for this very reason that though he had every opportunity to wrest kingly power, he maintained the simplicity befitting him. In fact, not even the former deeds alone, nor even those that that came later, which were far superior, went to his head. Of what kind were these? "David was prudent in all his ways," the text says, "and the Lord almighty was with him. All Israel loved David because he was at their head in marching out and returning. Saul's daughter Michal and all Israel loved him. David was wiser than Saul's servants, and his name was held in great honor. Saul's son Jonathan was very fond of David." [13] Yet despite his winning over all the populace and the king's household, prevailing in war in every case, never failing, and receiving such wonderful rewards for those good deeds, he was not puffed up, nor did he aspire to the kingship or take vengeance on his foe; instead, he continued to do him favors and had success in wars for his sake.

What person would be so savage and fierce that these deeds would not persuade him to set aside his enmity and rid him of his malice? Yet none of them convinced that cruel and inhumane man: blind to it all and surrendering his soul to malice, he endeavored to do away with him. For doing what (which is worse and quite amazing)? Playing his harp and soothing his disturbed spirits. "David kept playing his harp every day. Saul had his spear in his hand; Saul picked up the spear and said, 'I shall smite David,' and it stuck in the wall. Twice David kept out of his way." [14] Surely you could not cite a degree of evil beyond that? Perhaps what came after: despite the recent repulse of the enemy, the whole city being won over, everyone making victory offerings, he tried to do away with his benefactor and savior and cause of those good things while he was playing his harp, nor did the thought of his kindness check his frenzy and obsession. Instead, in his wish to do away with him he fired his spear at him on one or two occasions – such (681) was the kind of reward with which he repaid him for the risks taken. And he did this often, not on one day only.

That holy man, by contrast, even after all this continued

attending to the other's welfare, putting himself in danger for his safety, taking his place in the battle line in all the wars, and preserving his own assailant at personal risk. He did nothing in word or deed to irritate that wild beast; rather, in everything he gave way and was obedient. Though not receiving the prize due for his victory, and instead deprived of the reward for dangers undergone, he still did not ever utter reproaches to the soldiers or to the king; after all, he was doing this not for human reward but in the hope of recompense from on high. What is remarkable is not only that he did not demand the reward but that on account of his deep humility he also declined what was given. I mean, when Saul despite all his attempts and machinations was unable to do away with him, he concocted a scheme in the form of marriage, and came up with a new kind of present and wedding gift. "The king desires no gift," the text says, remember, "except for vengeance to be taken on the king's enemies with a hundred of their foreskins." [15] What he meant is something like this: Slay a hundred men, and that will do for a wedding gift. Now, he said this in his desire to expose him to the enemy on the pretext of the marriage.

David, however, judging the affair from the viewpoint of his gentleness, declined the marriage, not on account of the risks or for fear of the enemy, but from considering himself unworthy of relationship with him, and said as much to his servants in these words, "Is it a light matter in your eyes to be related to the king by marriage? I am a man of lowly station and of no consequence." [16] The thing was actually his due, a reward and recompense for his labors; but he was so humble in heart that despite such great achievements, so conspicuous a victory and a promise made, he considered himself unworthy to accept the reward due to him. He came to this conclusion when on the point of being in further danger. After prevailing over the enemy and taking the king's daughter in marriage, once again "David was playing his harp, and Saul tried to strike him with his spear, and he struck; but David got out of the way, and he stuck the spear in the wall." [17]

Would anyone, even the most philosophical, not be moved to anger by this, and apart from anything else would it not convince them in their concern for their safety to do away with the unjust schemer? This action would no longer be murder, you see: even by such an action he would have excelled the norm of the Law in force at that time. It provided, remember, for an eye being gouged out for an eye; even had he killed him, he would have committed one homicide for three, the three homicides having no reasonable grounds. He took no such course, however: he chose to flee, to be an exile from his ancestral home, be a refugee, take to his heels, and in a most wretched condition forage for his basic nourishment rather than be responsible for the king's execution. His interest, you see, was not in how to avenge himself but how to rid him of that malady. [18] The reason for withdrawing himself from his enemy's sight was to bring down the swelling, check the inflammation and allay the malice. It is better for me, he said, to be in a wretched state (682) and suffer countless wrongs than be convicted by God of this unlawful killing.

Let us not only hear this, but also imitate it, and let us put up with doing and suffering everything so as to rid our foes of their hostility towards us. Let us be interested not in whether it is fairly or unfairly that they are hostile to us, but in this alone – how they may no longer be at odds with us. This, after all, is the physician's interest, how to relieve the patient of the complaint, not whether they contracted the ailment fairly or unfairly. So you are a physician for the one who injures you: be interested in one thing only, how to remove their ailment. That is what this blessed man did, too, preferring poverty to riches, foreign parts to homeland, troubles and dangers to easy living and security, unending flight to staying at home so that he might rid the other man of hostility and enmity towards him.

Even so, however, Saul was not improved: he continued to pursue him, and went about in all directions in his efforts to find the one who had done him no wrong but had been gravely wronged and had repaid him for these wrongs with countless goods. All unawares he then actually fell into David's clutches. "There was a cave there," the text says, remember, "and Saul went in to relieve himself. David and his men were inside the cave. David's men said to him, 'Here is the day, just as the Lord said, I shall give your enemy into your hands, and you shall do with him what is pleasing in your sight.' David got up and secretly cut off the corner of Saul's cloak. Later David's heart smote him for cutting off the corner of the cloak, and David said to the men, 'God forbid that I should do this thing to my lord, the Lord's anointed, to raise my hand against him, for he is the Lord's anointed.'" [19]

Do you see the net spread, the prey snared, the hunter ready, everyone calling on him to plunge his sword in the enemy's breast? Note then, I ask you, the sound values, note the struggle, the victory, the crown: that cave was an arena, and a kind of remarkable and surprising contest took place. I mean, David entered the lists, resentment struck a blow, Saul was the prize, and God acted as referee – or, rather, the battle was not only against himself and his passions but also against the soldiers present: even if he chose to act on sound values and spare his assailant, it was likely he was also afraid they might slay him in the cave for undermining and betraying their safety and saving the life of their common foe. Each of them, in other words, was probably disgruntled and had in mind to say, We have become refugees and fugitives, and have been made exiles from home and country and everything else, and have shared all your troubles; you have in your grasp the cause of all these evils, and yet do you intend to let him off, with the result that we shall never have relief from these evils, and in your anxiety to save your foe you would betray your friends? How is this fair? If you have no concern for your own safety, spare our lives. Does what has happened not grieve you? do you not even remember what you suffered at his hands? For the sake of the (683) future take his life lest we suffer worse evils of greater magnitude. Even if they did not put this into words, you see, they nevertheless pondered it in their minds along with other more serious matters.

That righteous man, however, took none of these considerations into account: he focused on one thing only, how to succeed in winning the crown of forbearance and demonstrate sound values of a novel and extraordinary kind. You see, it would not have been so remarkable if while alone and by himself he had spared the aggressor as it is now extraordinary that he did so with others in his company, the presence of those soldiers proving a double obstacle to his sound values. In our case, for example, it often happens that we decide to dismiss our resentment and pardon someone their faults; but when we see people stirring us up and urging us on, we cancel our decision under influence of their words. This blessed man, however, was not affected like that: he continued to maintain his resolution even in spite of exhortation and advice. What is remarkable is not only that he was not swayed by the counsels of others and was not afraid of them, but that he also brought them round to his sound position. After all, while it is no mean thing for someone to get the better of their own passions, it is far greater to succeed also in convincing others to entertain the same attitude – especially when these others are not mild and moderate people but soldiers drilled in fighting, rendered desperate by the multitude of hardships, longing to rest a little, and aware that the solution to their problems depends completely on the killing of the enemy at that moment. And not only the solution to their problems, but also the attainment of countless goods: there was nothing to prevent the kingship passing to him as soon as the other man was killed. Still, despite so many soldiers urging him on, this noble man was able to prevail over them all, and to persuade them to pardon the enemy. [20]

It is worth listening to the advice of the soldiers: the malice in their advice brings out the righteous man's resolution and inflexibility. They did not even say, note, See, the one who contrives countless evils against you, who longed for your death, who beset us with irreparable difficulties. Instead, since they understood that he took no account of all such things and set no great store by the wrongs done to him, they adduced the judgement given him from on high in the words, "God has surrendered him," so that out of regard for the judgement from that quarter he might come more readily to the execution. Their meaning was, Surely you will avenge yourself? You serve and minister to God, and ratify his verdict. The more they said this, however, the more he was determined to spare him, knowing that God had given him into his hands so as to provide him with an opportunity for proving himself more fully.

In your case, then, when you see your enemy fall into your hands, consider it to be an occasion not for punishing but for saving. Hence the time of particular need for sparing (684) enemies is when they are in our power. But perhaps you may respond, What is wonderful and marvelous about sparing someone who is in our power? There are numerous cases of many other kings who succeeded to the throne and laid hands on their previous aggressors, but who thought it unworthy of them in their high position to settle scores; and so their sublime position proved a basis for reconciliation. In the present situation, however, you could not say anything similar applied: it was not a case of his succeeding to the throne, enjoying kingly rule and, with Saul in his hands, sparing him lest anyone should claim that the greatness of his position had dissipated his anger. Rather, though he was aware that on being spared he would get up to his old tricks and expose him to greater dangers, he still did not take his life. Let us not compare him with those others: having a secure pledge of future safety, they were right to show mercy, whereas in his case he was on the point of letting go someone hostile to him and saving the life of his own foe, and still did not eliminate him, despite having many factors urging him to commit the murder. [21] I mean, Saul's lack of helpers, the soldiers' urging, the recollection of past events, fear of what would happen, killing his foe not being judged in future as murder, his being able to surpass the requirements of the Law after the execution, and many other factors more convincing than these exercised force and pressure on him to wield the sword against him. To none of these pressures did he yield, however: he stood firm like some immovable object, preserving the norm of sound values inflexibly.

Then, in case you should claim that he experienced nothing of the kind normally felt, and that what was happening was insensitivity, not sound values, consider how he showed restraint though sorely tried. The fact, you see, that though the billows of resentment buffeted him and a great tempest of thoughts was stirred up, he held the storm in check with the fear of God and subdued his thinking you can see from what follows. "He got up," the text says, remember, "and secretly cut off the corner of Saul's cloak." Do you see how great the storm of resentment that was stirred up? Yet he proceeded no further, and did not commit shipwreck: the steersman was quickly on the alert – godly thinking – and produced calm in place of a storm; "his heart smote him," and he reined in his anger like a bucking and frenzied horse. This is what the souls of holy people are like: before falling they get up, before proceeding to sin they get a grip on themselves since they are watching and always on the alert. You might ask, what difference is there between flesh and clothing? All the same, he was strong enough not to proceed further, and he condemned himself severely even for that. "His heart smote him.," the text says, remember, "for cutting off the corner of the cloak, and he said to his men, 'The Lord forbid.'" What is the meaning of "The Lord forbid"? It means, May the Lord be merciful to me, and if I actually had the intention, may God not allow me to act on it nor permit me to proceed to the sin. In other words, since he knew that sound values of this kind (685) are almost beyond human nature and require grace from on high, and that he was halfway to committing murder, he then prays that God would keep his hand unstained.

What could be milder than this soul? Surely we shall not refer to this man as still human who while still belonging to human nature is giving evidence of the angelic way of life? The divine laws, however, would not permit.[22] After all, who would promptly choose, tell me, to make such a prayer to God? Why do I say, Such a prayer? Who would quickly bring himself not to pray against his aggressor? I mean, most people would be so much in the grip of ferocity that in case of weakness and inability to do their aggressor any harm they would call on God for vengeance and beseech him to allow them to avenge themselves on the wrongdoers. This man, by contrast, made his prayer in a directly opposite way to them, beseeching him not to allow him to avenge himself, expressing himself this way, "The Lord forbid that I should raise my hand against him," speaking of the enemy as though a son, as though a noble child.

He not only spared him, but even develops excuses for him. See how understanding and wise he is: although in a survey of his life he found nothing good, and could not claim, I have not been wronged by him or suffered any abuse (the soldiers present, after all, were ready to contradict this, knowing his wickedness from experience), he went about it in another way in his search for a face-saving defence. Then, failing to achieve this on the basis of his life and his actions, he had recourse to his status, saying, "Because he is the Lord's anointed." He means, What are you saying? That he is abominable, utterly abominable, reeking of countless crimes, and guilty of utter malice against us? Nonetheless, he is king, he is ruler, he has been entrusted with presiding over us. Instead of calling him king, what did he say? "Because he is the Lord's anointed," lending him respect not on the basis of his position here-below but of the decision from on high. He means, Are you showing scant respect for your fellow slave? respect the Lord. Do you despise the one with the commission? Fear the one who commissioned him. After all, if we fear and dread these officers commissioned by the king, be they vicious, be they rapacious, be they violent, be they unjust and anything else at all, not despising them for their wickedness but apprehensive because of the dignity of the one commissioning them, much more should we do so in God's case. He has not yet dismissed him from his position, he means, nor made him a private citizen. So let us not invert the proper order or be at odds with God, but give practical evidence of that apostolic saying, "Because everyone who resists lawful authority opposes God's directive, and those who oppose it will bring condemnation on themselves." [23]

Now, he called him not only anointed but also his own lord. This is no ordinary way of thinking, applying to the enemy the terms of status and respect. The full significance of this very thing you could likewise see from what other people experience. The general run of people, for example, do not stop short at calling their enemies by direct and simple names, but use other names denoting a serious accusation – blood-stained, crazy, insane, witless, destructive – and by stringing together many other such names they address their enemies in this fashion. (686) To prove this I shall give you an example not from a distance but from close at hand, from Saul himself. He could not bring himself to call this holy man, at any rate, by his own name on account of his deep hostility;

instead, when a festival was being celebrated on some occasion, he made this enquiry, "Where is the son of Jesse?" [24] He used this name of him, partly out of hatred of his name, partly in the hope of damaging the righteous man's reputation by mention of his father's lowly estate, not realising that it is not the notoriety of one's parents but virtue of soul that normally makes one conspicuous and notable.

David, however, was not like that: he did not call him by his father's name, extremely lowly and despicable though the man was; nor did he use a simple and direct name of him, but one referring to his status, to his power, so innocent of any hostility was his soul. In your case, therefore, dearly beloved, imitate this man, and learn this lesson first, never to use scurrilous names of your foe, but respectful ones; should your mouth be in the habit of calling your aggressor by names that are respectful and betoken service, the soul on hearing this will learn from the tongue, become accustomed and undergo a change of heart towards him. The words themselves will be the best remedy for the heart's choler.

I have said this at this point, not only for us to commend him, but also for us to imitate him. Let each of us, then, imprint on our own hearts this story, inscribing constantly in our thoughts as though by hand the double cave, Saul sleeping inside, in the grip of sleep as though in fetters, exposed to the striking arm of the one who had been wronged by him; David standing over him as he slept, the soldiers present, urging him to execution; the blessed man showing his sound values and repressing the resentment felt by himself and the men, and defending the one responsible for such awful crimes. [25] Let us not only write this on our minds but also repeatedly discuss it with one another in our get-togethers; let us constantly revive the memory of this story both with our wives and with the children. [26] In fact, if you want to talk about a king, see, there is a king here; if about soldiers, about a household, about political affairs, you will find a great abundance of these things in the Scriptures. These narratives bring the greatest benefit: it is impossible – impossible, I say – for a soul nourished on these stories ever to manage to fall victim to passion. [27]

Lest we waste our time, then, and devote our lives idly to trifles and extravagances, let us learn the stories of these noble men, let us constantly discuss the events and the characters. If someone in the group insists on raising the topic of spectacles, or the races, or matters of no relevance to you, lead them off that subject and bring them round to this discussion. Thus, with soul purified and with enjoyment free from risk, we may render ourselves gentle and mild towards all our aggressors, and so depart this world with no enemies, and attain the eternal goods, thanks to the grace and lovingkindness of our Lord Jesus Christ, to whom be the glory forever. Amen. (687)

Homily Two

On the theme that it is a great good not only to practise virtue but also to praise virtue,
and that he raised a greater trophy in sparing Saul than in felling Goliath,
and that in doing this he benefited himself rather than Saul, and on the defence he offered to Saul.

While the other day [1] you commended David's forbearance, I admired you for your fondness and affection for David. You see, not only practising and emulating virtue but also commending and admiring those practising it brings us no little recompense, just as likewise not simply emulating vice but also commending those living in it is a source of no chance retribution – in fact (to make a remarkable observation), it is worse than for those living in wickedness. The proof that this is true Paul brings out in what he says: after listing every form of vice and accusing all who trample on God's laws, he went on to say of those very people, "They are aware of God's decree, that those who commit such things deserve to die, yet they not only do them but also give approval to the guilty ones – hence you have no excuse, mortal that you are."[2] Do you see that he spoke this way for the purpose of showing the latter to be worse than the former? After all, going so far as to commend sinners is a greater basis for punishment than sinning, and rightly so: this decision comes from a mindset that is corrupt and suffering an incurable ailment. You see, the one who condemns the sin after committing it will eventually succeed in recovering self-possession, whereas those who commend wickedness will deprive themselves of the cure that comes from repentance. And so it was right of Paul to demonstrate the latter to be worse than the former. Just as not only those who commit unseemly acts, therefore, but also those who commend them will share the same punishment as they, or even worse, so those who commend and admire good people will have a share in the crowns available to them. You can see the same thing likewise in Scripture: in speaking to Abraham God said, "I shall bless those who bless you, and I shall curse those who curse you."[3] You could see this also in the case of the Olympic games: not only the athlete bedecked with the crown nor the one enduring the hardship and effort, but also the victor's admirer takes no little satisfaction from that applause.

For this very reason I bless not only that noble man for his sound values but also you for your fondness for him: he fought and won and was crowned, while you commended the victory and thus left with no small part in the crown. For the pleasure to be keener and the benefit greater, then, come now, let us pass on to you the remainder of the story as well. After reporting the words in which he deprecated the execution, in fact, the historian went on to say, "he did not let them rise up and kill Saul,"[4] wishing to bring out both their lust for blood and his courage. Admittedly, there are many adversaries, even with the appearance of sound values, (688) who, though personally reluctant to take life, would choose to offer no opposition to those bent on taking life. David was not of that kind, however: as though in receipt of a deposit and intent on keeping an account of it, he not only did not lay hands on the enemy himself but he also prevented those wanting to do away with him, acting as an excellent sentry and bodyguard instead of enemy. And so you would not be wrong to say it was David rather than Saul who at that moment was at risk. It was in fact no chance contest in which he was engaged in his efforts to extricate him by any means from their plans, nor was he as afraid of the likelihood of his being executed as he was afraid of one of the soldiers at one time being overcome with anger and slaying the fellow. Hence his devising such a rationale: they did the accusing while the accused man slept through it, whereas the enemy was defended, God made his decision and awarded the verdict to David.

It was not without God's influence, you see, that he succeeded in prevailing over those frenzied men: the grace of God was found on the inspired man's lips, adding a sort of inducement to those words. It was, however, no slight contribution that David also made:[5] since he had formed them in the past, consequently in the critical moment he found them ready and willing. It was not as leader of troops, you see, but as priest he commanded them, and that cave was a church on that occasion: like someone appointed as bishop, he delivered a homily to them, and after this homily he offered a kind of remarkable and unusual sacrifice, not sacrificing a calf, not slaying a lamb, but – what was of greater value than these – he offered to God gentleness and clemency, sacrificing irrational resentment, slaying anger and mortifying the limbs that are on the earth. He acted as victim, priest and altar: everything came from him – the thought that offered gentleness and clemency, the clemency and gentleness and the heart in which they were offered.[6]

When he had offered this excellent sacrifice, then, achieved the victory and omitted nothing needed for a trophy, the cause of the problem, Saul, arose and left the cave, all unaware of what had gone on. "David also left behind him,"[7] looking in the direction of heaven with eyes now free of concern, and more satisfied on that occasion than when he had overthrown Goliath and cut off the savage's head. It was, in fact, a more conspicuous victory than the former one, the spoils more majestic, the booty more glorious, the trophy more commendable: in the former case he needed sling, stones and battle line, whereas in this case thought counted for everything, the victory was achieved without weapons, and the trophy was erected without blood being spilt. He returned, therefore, bearing not a savage's head but resentment mortified and rage unnerved – spoils he deposited not in Jerusalem but in heaven and the city on high. In which case it was not women who came out to meet him, dancing and welcoming him with plaudits; (689) instead, the ranks of angels acclaimed him, marveling at his sound values and simplicity. He returns, after all, having dealt the enemy countless wounds, saving Saul's life, on the one hand, and on the other goading the real enemy, the devil, with many blows. You see, just as that creature is happy and joyous when we are resentful and quarrelsome and at odds with one another, so when we have peace and harmony and control our resentment, he is in turn checked and humbled, being an enemy to peace, a foe to harmony, and father of envy.

David emerged, therefore, his right hand bearing as a wreath the head that was equal in value to the whole world: just as in the case of the best contestants the emperors often wreathed the right hand of the boxer or wrestler instead of their head, so God too wreathed that right hand which succeeded in drawing the sword unbloodied, displaying to God the blade unstained, and resisting such a powerful flood of resentment. [8] He did not emerge with Saul's crown, but he emerged with a wreath of righteousness; he did not emerge with the purple mantle of royalty, but he emerged clad in clemency that surpassed human nature, a garment more resplendent than any robe. He left the cave with such wonderful splendor as the three young men left the furnace: [9] just as the fire did not consume them, so too the fire of resentment did not waste this man. In their case the fire on the outside did not come into contact with them, whereas he had the coals burning inside but saw the devil as a burning furnace on the outside – at the sight of his foe, the urging of the soldiers, the ease of achieving the execution, the absence of helpers, the memory of past injuries, the pressure of future ones (which enkindled a brighter flame than the kindling, pitch, tow and everything else that set the Babylonians' furnace alight) – yet he did not catch fire or undergo what you might expect; instead, he emerged unaffected, and despite getting a view of the enemy, he was the wiser for it. I mean, when he saw him sleeping and lying inert, [10] and incapable of doing anything, he said to himself, Where is that rage now? where the evil disposition? where those awful wiles and schemes? They have all vanished and been brought to nought with the mere onset of slumber, and the king lies in our power, without our planning or doing anything about them. He saw him sleeping, and pondered the common death of all: sleep is nothing other than temporary death and daily passing.

It would not be out of place for you to recall Daniel at this point: just as he got out of the pit, having prevailed over the wild beasts, so this man likewise emerged from the cave, getting the better of other worse wild beasts. I mean, just as lions were placed at various points around the former man, so too this man was beset by passions, lions fiercer than any others – (690) in one case resentment for past wrongs, in another dread of future ones – yet he held the beasts in check and shut their mouths, teaching in action that nothing is safer than sparing the enemy, and nothing more risky than planning to avenge oneself and settle scores. [11] At any rate, the man with the intention of attacking was in the position of someone alone and unarmed and destitute of everything, like a captive in enemy hands, whereas the other man gave way and yielded, not even choosing to attack with right on his side, innocent of schemes, weapons, horses and soldiers, and yet he had the enemy in his power – and what was most wonderful of all, he won God over to greater favor.

I declare that holy man blessed, you see, not because he saw his foe prostrate under his feet, but because he spared him when he had him in his grasp: one was the effect of God's power, the other of his own sound values. What likelihood was there that the soldiers would heed him? how well were they disposed towards him? If they had countless lives, would they not have readily offered them all for their leader, knowing from experiencing his care for the foe his benevolence for his own? After all, if he was gentle and mild towards those who did him harm, much more was he likely to be similarly disposed towards those who were on his side – the greatest pledge of security for him. They were not only more benevolent but even more enthusiastic in regard to their enemies, knowing they had God fighting on their behalf, who was always at their leader's side and made light of all their exploits. They gave heed to David, no longer as a mere mortal, but as an angel. Even before God's reward he personally reaped greater benefit here and now than the one whose life was spared, and he won a more illustrious victory than if he had slain Saul. After all, would he have gained so much by killing his enemy as he achieved by sparing his life?

Give thought to this yourself, [12] then, when you have in

your power the one who harmed you, that sparing is much more worthwhile and advantageous than killing: the one who kills will in many cases also condemn himself and have a bad conscience, each day and each hour haunted by that sin, whereas the one who spares and bears up for a short time will later rejoice and exult, expecting realisation of their hopes and looking forward to reward for forbearance from God. Should such people ever fall foul of some trouble, they will with great confidence look to God for recompense, just as likewise this man also enjoyed all this, eventually receiving generous and remarkable rewards from God for looking after this enemy of his.

Let us, however, see what happened later as well. "David left the cave behind Saul," the text says, "and called out after him in these words, 'My lord the king.' Saul looked back at him, and David bowed with his face to the ground, and paid homage." [13] This reflects no less credit than saving his foe: it is the mark of no ordinary soul not to be puffed up with favors conferred on the neighbor – or, rather, not to react like the general run of people, who despise and look down on the recipients of their favors as if they were menials. (691) Blessed David did not behave like that: he showed greater restraint even after the favor conferred. Now, the reason was that he did not attribute any of these achievements to his own initiative, ascribing it all to divine grace. [14] Hence, though he is the one who saved his life, he it is who pays homage to the one saved, calls him king and refers to himself as slave, by this deportment repressing his conceit, assuaging his resentment, and removing his envy.

Let us listen also to the defence itself. "'Why do you listen to the people's words that say, See, David is bent on taking your life?'" The historian in fact said previously to this that all the people were with him, he was pleasing in the eyes of the king's slaves, and the ruler's son and all the army were aligned in their loyalties with him. How, then, does he say here that there were slanderers and trouble-makers provoking Saul? Because, in fact, he was not misled by others, but gave rise to this malice of himself and proved hostile to the righteous man; the writer of the book indicated as much in saying that the envy was born of the plaudits and grew as each day passed [15] – hence his shifting the blame to others in the words, "'Why do you listen to your people's words that say, See, David is bent on taking your life?'" so as to give him the opportunity of repelling the malice. Parents, for example, also often do this with their children: one such takes his child aside, who has gone wrong and committed many faults, and even if he happens to be convinced that the child was drawn to vice of his own volition, he nonetheless in many cases shifts the blame for his faults on to others, speaking in these terms, I know it is not your fault, other people corrupting you and leading you astray, the blame being completely theirs. On hearing this, the child will gradually succeed in turning his gaze from vice and more easily return to virtuous ways, too ashamed and embarrassed to appear unworthy of this encomium. Paul also did as much in writing to the Galatians; at any rate, after those many lengthy words and indescribable accusations leveled at them, towards the end of the letter in his wish to dismiss the accusation against them so that they might gradually recover from their faults and succeed in mounting a defence, he spoke this way, "I am confident that you will be of no other mind; but the one who is confusing you will pay the penalty, whoever they be." [16]

This is what David also did in this case: the remark, "'Why do you listen to the people's words, See, David is bent on taking your life?'" brought out that other people were provoking him, other people corrupting him, his concern being to provide a defence against the charges. Then in defence against the charges leveled at him he said, "'See, today your eyes have witnessed that the Lord gave you into my hands in the cave, but I did not resolve to kill you; I spared you, saying, I will not lay a hand on my lord because he is the Lord's anointed.'" [17] In other words, while those others slandered him, he said, I shall mount a defence in actions, and in deeds I shall dispose of the accusation: there is no need of words, the very outcome of events succeeding in teaching more clearly than any word the sort of people they are and who (692) I am, and that the criticism made against me is slander and falsehood. In testimony to this I cite no one other than yourself, a beneficiary of mine.

How was the man in a position to testify (he is implying)? After all, when this happened, he was asleep, he neither heard the words nor saw David standing by and debating with the soldiers. So what position are we to adopt for the proof to be convincing? You see, if he had produced people who were with him at the time, Saul would have suspected their testimony and judged they were doing the righteous man a favor by saying this. If, on the other hand, he had endeavored to mount a defence by arguments and rationalisation, he would have been even more likely to disbelieve him, the judge's disposition already being biased. After all, how could the one who despite so many kindnesses was hostile to the man who had done him no harm come to believe that the wronged man had the wrongdoer in his hands and spared him? I mean, in most cases the general run of people form opinions about others on the basis of their own situation – for instance, the persistent drunkard would not readily believe that someone lives in sobriety, the patron of whores thinks those of spotless life are licentious, and likewise the one who purloins other people's property would not easily be convinced that there are people who even give away their possessions. [18] This man likewise, once he fell victim to resentment, would not easily have believed that someone could so prevail over passion as not only to do no wrong but even to save the life of the wrongdoer.

Since, then, the judge's will was corrupted, and witnesses,

had they been produced, would have been likely to fall under suspicion, he arranged for a proof to be given capable of reducing to silence even the most shameless. Of what kind was it? The corner of the cloak, which he actually produced and said, "'See, the corner of the cloak in my hand, which I removed, without killing you.'"[19] Voiceless the witness, but clearer than those with voice: if I were not close to you (he is saying), and standing near your person, I could not have cut part of your clothing. Do you see how much good came from David's being moved at the beginning? I mean, had he not been moved to resentment, we would not have come to know his sound values (most people would have got the impression that the sparing was the result not of sound values but of amazement), nor would he have cut off the corner; and not having cut it off, he would have had no other means to convince his foe. As it was, however, having been moved and done the cutting, he produced irrefutable proof of his care.

So since he produced true and unambiguous witness, he then calls on his foe in person as both judge and witness of his own solicitude, putting it this way, "'Be under no mistake and see clearly today that at my hand there is no evildoing or disrespect, and yet you are keeping my life in bondage so as to lay hold of it.'"[20] Here you might be particularly impressed by his magnanimity in that he mounted his defence only on the basis of what happened that day, implying this by saying, "'Be under no mistake and see clearly today.'" I make no mention of past events, he is saying: the present day suffices as proof for me. Admittedly, he could have cited many great kindnesses conferred previously, (693) had he wanted; for instance, he could have recalled the single-handed combat against the savage himself and said, When the war against the savages was on the point of sweeping away the whole city like a flood, and you were in fear and trembling and expecting to die any day, I issued forth, with no one pressuring me but with you opposing and restraining me in the words, "'You cannot go, because you are a stripling, whereas he has been a man of war from his youth.'" [21] Instead of hanging back, I lept forward ahead of all the others, took the enemy on, cut off his head, checked the attack of those savages like some tempestuous torrent, and stopped the city tottering. It is on account of me that you have your kingship and your life, and everyone now has city and homes, children and wives along with their lives. He could have mentioned likewise after that the trophy, other wars he successfully waged no less important than that. The fact that he had tried on many an occasion to do away with him, and had aimed a spear at his head, he did not bring up, nor the fact that after that, when he was due to make a repayment for the former battle, he had looked for a gift, not of gold or silver, but his own slaughter and overthrow – even in this case he did not object. All this, in fact, and much more of greater importance he could have mentioned, but he mentioned none of it: he had no wish to throw his kindnesses in his teeth – only to persuade him that he was among the number of those who loved and cared for him, not of those who schemed and warred against him.

Hence he left all those matters aside, and adduced for the purposes of his defence only what happened that very day. He was so modest and free of all vainglory, and had eyes on one thing only, God's verdict. Then he said, "'Let the Lord judge between me and you.'" [22] He uttered this remark, not out of a desire for the man to be punished or receive retribution from him, but to frighten him with the mention of the judgement to come – and not only frighten him but also mount a defence in his own case. It is even from my actions in particular that I have proof, he is saying, but if you are not convinced, I call God himself as witness, who knows the unspoken thoughts of each one's mind and can discern their conscience. Now, he said this to bring out that he would not have summoned the judge who is beyond deception and brought him to judgement on him had he not been quite convinced that he was free of all guile.

The fact that the words were not a ploy, and instead in his wish to mount a defence in his own case and his desire to bring him to his senses he referred to that judgement, is indicated sufficiently by what had already occurred; what happened later, however, can confirm it no less than that. Having him in his hands, remember, when despite that rescue he was still inveighing against him and wanting to do away with him, and though being in a position to cut him down along with his whole army, he let him go without any of the evil effects he would normally have suffered. Hence, when he realised that his complaint was incurable and he would never cease his hostility towards him, he withdrew himself from his eyes, and lived among the savages, in service, without honor, in a shameful condition, foraging for the necessities of life by labor and hardship.

This is not the only remarkable thing: (694) on hearing that he fell in battle he rent his garments, scattered dust on himself and gave way to a lament you would utter if you had lost a true and only child, continually calling on his name along with his son, composing eulogies, uttering bitter cries, fasting till evening, and cursing the very place that had taken the blood of Saul. "'Mountains of Gilboa,'" he said, remember, "'may no dew or rain fall upon you; mountains of death, because it is there that shelter of the powerful has been snatched away.'" [23] As often happens with parents, shunning their home and glancing sorrowfully on the street along which they followed the funeral of their child, so did this man behave, cursing the mountains that had been the site of the slaughter. I hate even the very place on account of those who have fallen there, he is saying; no longer rain on it, therefore, with showers from on high: once you were evil enough to rain the blood of my friends. Over and over he invoked their names without ceasing, speaking in these terms, "'Saul and Jonathan, beloved and comely, never apart in their life, and not separated in their death.'" [24] Since their bodies could not be embraced, you see, he enfolds them in these names, assuaging his grief with them, as far as possible, and mitigating the enormity of the disaster. I mean, though many thought that the fact that both died on the one day was an unmitigated disaster, he took this very thing as grounds for comfort: his saying, "'never apart in life, and not separated in their death,'" came from someone interpreting it as nothing but this. It cannot now be claimed, he is saying, that the son lamented his being an orphan nor the father grieved for his childlessness: what happened to no one happened to them, he is saying, on the one day being snatched from life together, neither left behind. In his view, you see, life would have been unlivable with the separation of one from the other.

Are you upset at this, are you weeping, your thoughts confused, and your eyes turned readily to the shedding of tears? [25] Let each of you, I ask you, recall the one who has been hostile and harmful, your mind still affected by grief; cherish them while alive and lament them when deceased, not for display but with true mind and soul. Even if you have to put up with something to avoid harming the wrongdoer, take every step and put up with it, looking to God for a great reward. See, at any rate, this man: he gained the kingship without staining his hand with blood and instead keeping his right hand undefiled, and thus he was awarded the crown and ascended the throne, his sparing the foe and lamenting the fallen proving for him a more conspicuous basis for praise than purple and diadem. [26] Because of this the memory is preserved not only of his life but also of his death. And so if you, too, wish to attain lasting glory, mortal that you are, and to enjoy in that place imperishable goods, imitate the righteous man's virtue, emulate his sound values, give evidence in practice of (695) this forbearance of his so that by enduring the same hardships as his you may be considered worthy of the same good things. May it be the good fortune of us all to attain this, thanks to the grace and lovingkindness of our Lord Jesus Christ, to whom with the Father and the Holy Spirit be glory, power and honor, now and forever, for ages of ages. Amen.

Homily Three

On the fact that attendance at spectacles is dangerous,
that it produces accomplished adulterers,
and is the cause of depression and hostility,
that David surpassed every form of forbearance
in his dealings with Saul,
and that bearing robbery mildly is on a par with giving alms.

I am inclined to think that many of those who abandoned us the other day and took their leave for spectacles of an unlawful character are here today.[1] I would like to be clear as to who they are so as to put them beyond the sacred doors, not for them to remain outside perpetually, but to come back again when they have been corrected. Parents frequently expel from home children who have gone wrong and exclude them from table, not to banish them forever, but for them to be made better by this chastisement and return to their ancestral home with due decorum. Shepherds also do it, excluding sheep affected by mange from the healthy ones so that they may get rid of the wretched disease and come back again to the healthy ones in safety, and that the sick ones may not infect the whole flock with that plague.

This is, to be sure, the reason that we also want to know these people. Even if, however, we fail to discern them with our bodily eyes, the homily will identify them perfectly, and by laying hold of their conscience it will easily persuade them to depart willingly, making clear that that person alone belongs inside here who has an attitude that is worthy of converse here, as the person of corrupt lifestyle taking part in this sacred assembly, even if bringing their body here, has been expelled, and is excluded to a greater extent than those shut out and not yet able to share the sacred banquet. [2] The former people, you see, who have been expelled in keeping with God's laws and remain outside, have in the meantime sound hope: if they want corrected the sins for which they find themselves outside the church, they will be able with purified conscience to come back again. Those who have defiled themselves, on the contrary, and are bidden not to enter before being cleansed of the stain of their sins, then by their shamelessness make the wound worse and the ulcer more serious: sinning is not so serious as shamelessness after the sin and not obeying the priests giving such orders. What sin has been committed by these people of such gravity, you ask, as to expel them from the sacred precincts? What other kind of sin are you looking for more serious than this, when having turned themselves into accomplished adulterers they betake themselves, without a qualm, like mad dogs, to this sacred banquet?

If you want to learn as well the style of this adultery, I shall cite to you not a word of mine but of him who is going to judge the whole of our lives. "The one who looks at a woman with lust," Scripture says, remember, (696) "has already committed adultery with her in his heart." [3] Take the case of a woman who by accident happens to be in the marketplace and in her casual dress chances to catch the attention of the man with a roving eye. Those who not idly or by chance, but of such set purpose as to scorn the Church, go there for the very purpose and spend the day there, obsessed with the sight of those shameless women – how will they manage to claim that they were not looking with lust? Where the talk is outrageous, the songs lewd, the lyrics seductive, eyes highlighted, cheeks rouged, dress designed for the purpose, appearance oozing beguilement, and many other tricks designed for deceiving and ensnaring the spectators; where there is spiritual sloth in the onlookers, complete confusion, an appeal to licentiousness in the surroundings, in the sounds beforehand and those that come later, the bewitching music of pipes, of flutes and of other such instruments, undoing the mind's resolve, exposing the spirits of the patrons to the blandishments of the whores and making them more vulnerable. [4] I mean, if in this place, where there are psalms, prayers and attention to the divine sayings, lust frequently gains entry by stealth like some cunning brigand, how would those reclining at the theatre, seeing nothing or hearing nothing wholesome, and only awash with utter shamefulness, utter stupidity, and under pressure from all sides by eye and by ear, succeed in being beyond the reach of that evil lust? Failing to do it, how will they succeed in ever being rid of the charges of adultery? And those not rid of the charges of adultery – how will they succeed in approaching these sacred doors without repentance and participating in this fine assembly?

Hence I beg and implore you to cleanse yourself first by abasement [5] and repentance and every other means from the sin of the spectacle in that place, and thus attend to the divine sayings. After all, this is no slight fault on our part; you could recognise this clearly even from parallels. If, for example, into your closet, where there are kept the owner's clothes rich and golden in material, a servant wore a garment all filthy and grubby, I ask you, surely you would not take kindly to the disrespect? And if someone poured dung and mire into a golden vase usually containing perfumes, would you not actually beat the one guilty of this? Then shall we take such care of closets and vessels and garments and perfumes while not regarding our soul to be more elevated than all these? And where the spiritual perfume is poured would we introduce devilish processions, satanic tales and ditties oozing impurity? Tell me, how would God take this? Actually, there is not such a difference between perfume and mire, masters' garments and slaves', as between spiritual grace and this evil activity. Are you not terrified, mortal that you are, to gaze with the same eyes both on the bed on the stage, where (697) the loathsome rites of adultery are performed, and on this sacred table, where the awesome sacraments are enacted? to listen with the same ears both to shameful depravity and to Old and New Testament readings schooling you in the mysteries? to make the same heart recipient of both the baleful potions and the awesome and holy victim?[6]

Is not the former place the source of ruined lives, broken marriages, squabbles and wrangles in homes? I mean, when you are dissipated with the spectacle there, and become more dissolute and lecherous and resistant to any self-control, on returning home and seeing your wife, it is altogether a more disagreeable prospect, no matter what she is like: aflame with the lust arising from the spectacles, and enthralled by that novel and beguiling experience, for your chaste and comely partner sharing your whole life you have only scorn and abuse, and inflict on her countless taunts, having nothing to reproach her with but ashamed to mention your problem and display the wound you came back home with. You concoct numberless pretexts, looking for irrational grounds for hostility, scorning everything at home while pining for that loathsome and filthy object of desire by which you have been smitten. With the deafening sound of that voice fixed in your soul, as well as the whore's appearance and gaze and movements, and every image of her, you find nothing at home a pleasure to look upon.

Why mention wife and home? The church itself, in fact, you will find a more disagreeable sight, and will have some resistance to the preaching on self-control, on sobriety. In your case, in fact, the words will be not instruction but accusation, and you will gradually be reduced to despair and eventually remove yourself from this instruction meant for the good of all. Hence I beg you all to shun both the wicked dallying at the shows and those who have the time to be attracted to them there: all that happens there is not entertainment but ruin, retribution and punishment. After all, what is the good of this passing pleasure when the pain arising from it is unending, and day and night you are goaded by lust, disgruntled and out of sorts with everything? Examine yourself, therefore, as to what sort of person you are when you leave the church and what you are like when you leave the spectacles: compare the different days, and you will have no need of words from us, comparison of the two days sufficing to bring out the magnitude of the benefit gained here and the harm sustained there.

I have already mentioned this to you, dearly beloved, and shall never cease mentioning it: we shall both admonish those suffering this awful complaint and render the healthy more secure. Our sermon, you see, is of benefit to both groups – to the former that they may desist, to the latter lest they fall victim. Since, however, those who chide should do so in moderation, let us bring our exhortation to an end at this point, [7] and pass on to you what remains of the former theme by going back to David once again. It is customary with painters, remember, when they intend to make a likeness of someone, for those due to be painted to stay close to them for a day or two or three so as to ensure faultlessly the precision of the likeness by the frequency of the sitting. (698) Since, then, it is our purpose to sketch not only the outline of his bodily form but the beauty and spiritual comeliness of his soul, we intend to have David sitting close to you today as well so that all of you may look at him and impress on your own souls individually the righteous man's comeliness, his gentleness and mildness, his magnanimity and every other virtue of his. [8] After all, if bodily images give some comfort to the onlookers, much more images of the soul. While the former cannot be looked at in every situation, and instead have to be set up in one place, there is nothing to prevent your taking the latter with you wherever you choose: by putting it in the recesses of your mind wherever you are, you can look at it constantly and reap much benefit from it. Just as those with eye problems hold on to sponges and cloths stained dark blue and look at them constantly, and get some relief for the complaint from that color, so too in your case, if you keep the image of David before your eyes and constantly gaze at it, even if time and time again resentment clouds and confuses the mind's eye, by looking on that image of virtue you will receive a complete cure and values that are sound and pure.

I mean, let no one say, I have a disgusting enemy, evil, corrupt, incorrigible. Whatever you come up with, they are no worse than Saul, who though saved on many an occasion by David, personally mounted schemes beyond number and still, despite being given favors in return for them, persisted in his wickedness. What claim can you make, after all? that they took a part of your land, did you harm in property matters, transgressed the boundaries of your house, stole your slaves, abused you, were greedy, reduced you to indigence? They still did not take your life, however, which was what that man was bent on; and if they were bent on taking your life, they perhaps tried it on one occasion, not over and over again like him; and if over and over again, they still were not in receipt of such favors, they still did not fall into your hands once or twice and have their lives spared; and even if this happened, David is still more generous. It is impossible, in fact, for someone in the Old dispensation to show such sound values, and now after the coming of grace to grant such wonderful favors. David had not heard the parable of the ten thousand talents and the hundred denarii;[9] David had not heard the prayer that says, "Forgive people their debts as your heavenly Father also does;"[10] he had not seen Christ crucified, not seen the precious blood poured out, not heard the countless words about sound values; he had not had the benefit of such a wonderful sacrifice, nor shared in the Lord's blood. Instead, he was raised on imperfect laws that made no such requirements, yet he attained to the very summit of sound values of the age of grace.

Whereas you are frequently resentful over past injuries and bear a grudge, he by contrast, though fearful of what was to come and fully aware that if (699) he saved the man's life the city would be out of bounds to him and life would be unlivable, did not desist from his care: he did everything to protect the one who was hostile to him. Who could cite greater forbearance than this?[11] For you to learn also from what happens in our day, however, that it is possible, if we are willing, to reconcile every person bearing hostility to us, what could be fiercer than a lion? Yet people tame it, skill gets the better of nature, and the beast that is more ferocious and more kingly than all others becomes milder than any sheep and moves through the marketplace causing terror to no one. So what excuse do we have, what pretext, for taming wild beasts but claiming people cannot be placated or brought to be well disposed to us? Actually, ferocity belongs to the beast by nature, whereas in a human being ferocity is contrary to nature; so when we prevail over nature, what excuse will we have for claiming free will cannot be corrected? If, however, you still object, I would reply that even should they prove to be afflicted with an incurable ailment, the greater the effort on your part, the greater will be the reward for you in your persistence and attention to the one incurably afflicted.

Let us concentrate on one thing, therefore, not on suffering no harm from our enemies, but on causing them no harm ourselves. We shall suffer no trouble even if we encounter innumerable troubles, just as David suffered none, though driven out, made a fugitive, the object of plots against life itself; instead, he was more illustrious and august than the other man, and more dear to everyone, not to human beings alone but also to God himself. After all, what harm came to that holy man from suffering such things from Saul at that time? are his praises not sung to this very day, is he not famous on earth and more famous in heaven? do not ineffable goods await him, even the kingdom of heaven? And, on the other hand, what good did that poor wretch achieve by those awful schemes of his? did he not lose the kingship, suffer a pitiable death along with his son, come under accusation by all and, what is worse, receive undying punishment? [12] In a word, what on earth is it that you have against your enemy that you are not prepared to be reconciled? He took your money? If you accept the loss nobly, you will receive as great a reward as if you lodged it in the hands of the poor. The one who gives to the poor, remember, and the one who does not plot and inveigh against the fraudulent both do this for God's sake. So since the motivation of the outlay is one and the same, it is clear that one and the same is the crown.

But did he not plot against my life and endeavor to do away with it? The affair is taken as martyrdom for you provided you number among your benefactors the schemer who took his hostility to this point, and keep praying for him, even calling on God to be merciful to him. Let us not get the impression, after all, that God prevented him from killing David; rather, let us consider that he won a three- or four-fold crown from Saul's scheming. You see, the one who saved the life of the enemy who on many an occasion (700) fired his spear at his head, and who was in a position to do away with him but then spared him, despite knowing that after being spared he would be up to his old tricks, was clearly slain countless times; but being slain countless times, he has many crowns for martyrdom. Paul also said as much, "I die daily for God's sake," [13] and even personally experienced it for God's sake. He was in a position to do away with the schemer, but for God's sake did not choose to; instead, he preferred to run the risk every day rather than be freed from such deaths by committing a justified homicide. Now, if at the risk to life itself it does not require taking vengeance on the schemer and hating him, much less on someone guilty of some casual wrongdoing.

Many people feel that being given bad reports and put under suspicion by their enemies is more intolerable than any death; so, come, let us examine this closely as well. Did someone speak badly of you and call you adulterous and lecherous? If they speak the truth, mend your ways; but if lies, laugh at them. If your conscience admits what is said, come to your senses; but if it does not, do not only scorn them but also rejoice and exult in keeping with the Lord's direction to that effect, "When they reproach you and say every evil thing against you falsely, rejoice and be glad that your reward in heaven is great;" [14] and again, "Rejoice and exult when they falsely black-list you." [15] Even if they are correct in what they say, and you take the words mildly, not abusing or reviling them but sighing bitterly and condemning your faults, you will reap no less a reward than before. I shall try to demonstrate this fact to you from the Scriptures for you to learn that the degree of benefit you fail to gain from friends' praise and compliments you do gain from enemies' derogatory remarks, even if they speak the truth, provided we are prepared to put the accusations to good use. Friends, you see, often flatter us to gain favor, whereas enemies bring our sins to the fore: since out of self-love we do not see our failings, in many cases they gain a more precise insight into us out of hostility, and by reproaching us they drive us on to the need for correction, and the hostility proves for us a source of the greatest benefit, not only because thanks to their reminder we understand our sins but because we also lay them aside. I mean, if your enemy reproaches you for a sin which your conscience acknowledges, and you sigh bitterly and beseech God, you have immediately set all sin aside. Surely there is nothing more blessed than that? what easier way is there for achieving freedom from sins?

In case, however, you think we are simply leading you on, I shall provide testimony on this from the divine Scriptures for you to be no longer in any doubt. There was a certain pharisee and a publican: one was (701) driven to the depths of evil, the other practised eminent righteousness, giving away his possessions, persevering in fasting, and innocent of greed, while the other man spent all his time in fraud and violence. Both went up to the Temple to pray; then the former stood up and said, "I give thanks to you, O Lord, that I am not like other people – rapacious and greedy – nor like this tax collector, either." [16] The tax collector, by contrast, stood at a distance, he did not hurl abuse or obloquy in return, he did not speak the words in use by the general run of people: Do you presume to make reference to my life, to criticise my actions? Am I not better than you? Let me tell you your sins, and I shall ensure you never enter these sacred precincts again. He said none of the heartless things we heap up on one another in our daily converse; instead, sighing bitterly and beating his breast, he made only this kind of remark, "Have mercy on me a sinner," [17] and went away in a righteous condition.

Do you see the promptitude? He accepted the reproach, and cleansed himself of the reproach; he acknowledged his sins, and put aside his sins; the accusation of sin proved the removal of sin, and his foe unwittingly turned benefactor. I mean, what effort would it have required for the tax collector to fast, sleep on the ground, keep vigil, give his goods to the needy, spend a long period sitting in dust and ashes so as to succeed in setting aside those sins? As it was, without doing anything of the sort, he set aside all his wickedness in a mere word; the reproaches and abuse of the one seeming to malign him won a crown of righteousness for him, without sweat or effort or length of time. Do you see that even if someone speaks the truth about us, even if they are the kinds of things we acknowledge to ourselves, and we do not abuse the speaker but sigh bitterly and make supplication to God for our sins, we shall succeed in setting aside all our faults? This, at any rate, was the way this man was made righteous: since he did not abuse the other man, and instead sighed over his own sins, the former it was who went away in a righteous condition rather than the latter.

Do you see the great advantage there is in the abuse from enemies, provided we take it in the right spirit? Since they are beneficial to us, whether telling lies or the truth, why do we get upset? why do we weep? If you do not bring harm on yourself, mortal that you are, no friend or foe or the devil himself will be able to harm you. In fact, since the abusers, the gossips, those whose schemes reach on life itself are to our benefit, and some weave for us a wreath of martyrdom, as we demonstrated, while others deplore our sins and make us righteous, as happened in the case of the tax collector, why do we rage against them? So let us not say, So-and-so provoked me, and so-and-so led me to say shameful things: we are responsible in every case for this. I mean, if we are prepared to exhibit sound values, not even a demon will be able to move us to anger; this is clear both from those other people and from the very story before us about David, which was worth bringing to your notice today as well before reminding your good selves of the point at which we lately drew our address to a close. [18]

At what point, then, did we bring it to a close? (702) At David's defence. So today we must mention Saul's response and see what reply he gave to the other man's self-justification: it is not only from the words David uttered but also from what Saul says that we shall see David's virtue. In fact, if he gives the impression of uttering anything gentle and mild, we shall attribute it to the one who changed him, who corrected and settled his soul. What, then, did Saul say? Having heard David saying, "See, here is the corner of your cloak in my hand," and everything else by which he mounted his defence along with this, he said, "Is this your voice, my child David?" [19] O, what a great change had suddenly taken place: the one who could never bear even to call him by name, and instead hated the very mention of it, even admitted him to kinship, calling him "child." What could be more blessed than David, who turned the murderer into a father, the wolf into a lamb, who filled the furnace of anger with heavy dew, turned the tempest into tranquillity and allayed all the inflammation of resentment? Those words of David, you see, penetrated the mind of that enraged man and effected this total transformation, as you can see from those words: he did not even say, Are these your words, my son David? but "Is this your voice, my child David?" He was now heartened by his very utterance: just as a father hears the voice of his son returning from somewhere and is excited not only at the sight of him but also at the sound of his voice, so Saul too, when David's words penetrated and drove out the hostility, now recognised him as holy, and in setting aside one passion he was affected by another. That is to say, by driving out resentment he was affected by benevolence and fellow feeling.

Just as when it is night we do not recognise even friends, whereas when day comes we know them on catching sight of them from a distance, this is also the way things normally happen in the case of hostility as well. As long as we are at odds with one another, we hear their voice differently and look upon their face with a jaundiced attitude, whereas when we set aside the resentment, their voice, previously hostile and inimical, strikes us as kindly and pleasant, and the sight of them, once hostile and distasteful, becomes desirable and graceful. This happens in the case of a storm as well: the mass of clouds does not allow the beauty of the sky to appear; instead, even if we have exceptionally keen sight, we are not able to penetrate through to the brightness above. But when the sun's warmth continues for a while and dissipates the gloom, it reveals the sun and makes clear also in due course the charm of the sky. This is what happens also in our feeling resentment: hostility acts as thick gloom before our eyes and ears, and makes sound and sight seem different; but when someone by applying sound values sets aside hostility and dissipates the gloom of sullenness, then everything is seen and heard with unaffected attitude. [20] (703)

Which was consequently Saul's experience: when he penetrated the gloom of hostility, he recognised David's voice, saying, "Is this your voice, my child David?" What sort of voice was "this"? The one that overthrew Goliath, snatched the city from danger, brought everyone in danger of slavery and death to safety and freedom again, repressed that man's frenzy, won for him many wonderful benefits. This, in fact, is the voice that overthrew that awful savage, the power of prayer subduing him before the stone did. He did not simply fire the stone, remember: he first said, "You advance on me with your gods, but I advance against you in the name of the Lord of hosts, whom you have reviled today," [21] and then he let fly. The voice guided the stone, it struck anguish into the savage, it despatched the enemy's bravado. Why are you surprised if a righteous person's voice represses resentment and destroys enemies when it even drives out demons? The apostles, for instance, had only to speak, and all the opposing forces took to their heels. The voice of holy people even stopped the elements in many cases, and altered their way of acting. Joshua son of Nun, for example, merely said, "Let the sun and the moon stand still," and they did; [22] Moses likewise held the sea in check and released it; [23] the three young men likewise extinguished the force of the fire by those hymns and the voice. [24]

Hence Saul, heartened at the sound of this voice, said, "Is this your voice, my child David?" So what did David reply? "Your servant, my lord the king." [25] A contest and rivalry then develop as to which one will pay greater respect to the other: one admitted the other to kinship, the other called him lord. What he means is something like this: I am interested in one thing only, your welfare and the progress of virtue; you called me child, and I love and am fond of you if you have me as a servant, provided you set aside your resentment, provided you do not suspect me of any evil or think me to be scheming and warring against you. He fulfilled that apostolic law, note, that bids us excel ourselves in showing one another honor, [26] unlike the general run of people, whose disposition is worse than beasts', and who cannot bear to be the first to greet their neighbor, having the view that they are shamed and insulted if they share a mere greeting with someone. What could be more ridiculous than this stupidity? what more shameful than this conceitedness and folly? I mean, then it is, mortal as you are, that you are insulted, then you are shamed, then you are dishonored, when you wait for your neighbor to greet you first. After all, what could be worse than folly? what more ridiculous than conceitedness and vainglory? You see, if you are the first to give the greeting, God gives the commendation, which is more important than all, people approve, and you yourself receive the whole reward for that greeting, whereas if you wait to be shown respect before showing it, you have then done nothing of any value: the one who took the initiative in showing respect will be the one to receive the whole reward for the attention shown him by you.

So let us not wait to be the first to be shown respect: let us hasten to pay respect to the neighbor and always take the initiative in greeting, and not think it a slight and trivial act of virtue, (704) being affable and affectionate in greeting others. When neglected, at any rate, it has broken many friendships, created many enmities, just as when studiously observed it has destroyed longstanding hostility and sealed existing friendships. So do not be found wanting, dearly beloved, in zeal for this; instead, if possible let us be the first to pay attention to those we meet, whoever they may be, both in greeting them and in all other respects. But if someone anticipates you, show them greater respect in return; Paul in fact urged this in saying, "Treat one another as superior to yourselves." [27]

This is what David did, being the first to show respect and, when shown it, showing greater respect in return, saying, "Your servant, my lord the king." See what great benefit he gained: when David said this, Saul could not bear any longer to hear this voice without weeping; instead, he cried out bitterly, revealing by his tears the soundness of spirit and the right values that David had instilled. What could be more blessed than the prophet's reforming his enemy in such a short space of time, winning over a soul thirsting for his blood and murder, and suddenly reducing him to laments and groans? I do not marvel as much at Moses for drawing torrents of water from the split rock as I marvel at David for drawing torrent of tears from stony eyes: the former overcame nature, the latter prevailed over free will; the former smote the rock with his rod, the latter struck the heart with his word, not to do damage but to render him pure and gentle – which in fact he did by giving greater evidence of kindness than before. While he deserves commendation and deep admiration for not staining his sword or cutting off that hostile head, yet his changing the man's very will, making him better and bringing him round to his own gentle ways would deserve far greater crowns. The latter favor was greater than the former: bestowing the gift of life does not match leading one to sound values; ridding one of resentment after his panting for unjust slaughter, stopping one from murder, and removing one from the frenzy that leads on to such an awful wrong are not of equal significance. I mean, stopping the bodyguards from doing away with him was a benefit of the present life, whereas banishing wickedness from the soul by mildness in speech conferred on him the future life and imperishable goods, at least as far as lay in him. So when you praise him for his characteristic gentleness, admire him to a greater extent for the change in Saul: a much greater achievement than controlling his own passions is his also prevailing over the frenzy of others, repressing an inflamed heart, effecting such calm after such an awful tempest, and filling eyes contemplating homicide with warm tears. This it is that is productive of deep astonishment and wonder: if Saul had been one of those mild and moderate people, it would not have been anything out of the ordinary to lead him to his own practice of virtue; but causing him in his enraged state, driven to extreme evil and bent on slaughter as he was, to extinguish all that bitterness in a flash (705) – is there anyone ever given notoriety for instruction in sound values whom this does not eclipse?

You, therefore, when you have your enemy in your power, do not make it your concern how to avenge yourself and after subjecting him to countless outrages get rid of him, but how to look after him, how to bring him to mildness; do not stop short of doing and saying everything until by gentleness you overcome his ferocity. Nothing, after all, is more efficacious than mildness; someone suggested as much in the words, "A soft tongue will break bones:" what could be tougher than bones, and yet should anyone be as tough and unbending as that, the one employing mildness will easily prevail. And again, "A submissive answer turns away wrath." [28] Hence it is clear that you have more say than your enemy in his being upset and his being reconciled: it is up to us, not to the wrathful, both to snuff out their resentment and to kindle the flame to greater heat. The previous authority suggested as much by a simple example, saying, Just as you ignite the flame by blowing on a spark, but extinguish it by spitting on it, and you have the say in each case (his words are "Both come out of your mouth"),[29] so too with hostility towards your neighbor: if you give vent to inflated and foolish words, you enkindle his fire, you ignite the coals, but if peaceable and moderate words, you extinguish his rage completely before the fire takes on. So do not say, I suffered this and this, I was told this and this: you have the say in it all; as with extinguishing and enkindling the fire, so with inflaming or repressing his resentment, it is likewise up to you.

When you see your enemy or have him in mind, forget all those harmful things you suffered or were told; if they still come to mind, put it down to the devil. Recollect, rather, whether he ever said or did anything useful to you; if you turn these things over in your mind, you will promptly dissolve your enmity. If you are on the point of calling him to account, first expel the strong feeling and snuff out the resentment, then require an account from him, then make your point, and you will easily succeed in staying in control. When we are angry, you see, we shall never succeed in saying or being told anything constructive, whereas when we are rid of that feeling, we ourselves shall never utter any harsh word or hear others speaking in such terms. It is not so much, in fact, the nature of what is said as our predisposition to hostility that generally annoys us; often, at any rate, when we hear the same things from friends who are joking or jesting, or even from small children, we not only do not take exception or fall into a rage, but we even laugh and are diverted, hearing it not with a twisted attitude or a mind predisposed to anger. And so, in the case of enemies as well, if you extinguish the resentment, if you expel the hostility, nothing said will succeed in harming you.

Why do I say, nothing said? Not even anything that happens (706) will harm you, just as it did not harm this blessed man, either: seeing the enemy taking arms against his safety and moving might and main to that end, he was not only not enraged but even felt for him more keenly; the more he plotted, the more he wept for him. He was aware, you see, he was well aware that it is not the object of evil but the doer of evil who deserves tears and laments for bringing harm on himself. Hence he directed a lengthy defence to him, and did not desist until he had caused him to offer a defence of himself with tears and laments. He gave vent, in fact, to wailing and bitter cries, and loudly lamented; listen to what he said: "You are more righteous than I, for you repaid me with good and I repaid you with evil." [30] Do you see how he condemns his own wickedness, praises the righteous man's virtue, and under no pressure from anyone apologises? Do likewise in your own case: [31] when you have your enemy in your power, instead of accusing him, apologise so as to bring him to accuse himself; if we make the accusation, he will be exasperated, whereas if we apologise, he will be impressed with our mildness and then accuse himself on his own initiative. In this way the charge is above suspicion, and he is freed from all malice.

Which is exactly what happened in this case: the wrongdoer accuses himself with great severity, the wronged man saying nothing. He did not simply say, note, "You did good to me," but "You repaid me with good" – in other words, in return for scheming, in return for violence, in return for those countless evils you repaid me with great kindnesses. But I did not become better from them; instead, I persisted in my wickedness despite those kindnesses; but instead of being changed, you persevered in maintaining your behavior and doing further kindnesses to us. How many crowns, then, would David have deserved for each of those words? After all, even if it was Saul's mouth that uttered them, yet it was David's wisdom and skill that planted them in his heart. "Today you informed me," he said, "of the good things you did for me in not killing me when the Lord this day imprisoned me in your grasp."[32] He gives him testimony to a further virtue as well, that after his benefactions he did not keep silence nor pass over them: he came forward and spoke of them, not doing so for the sake of ostentation but in his wish to bring out and teach from the deeds themselves that he was one of those who were caring and thoughtful, not those scheming and misbehaving. One may, you see, make mention of one's own beneficence when it results in benefit of the highest order. In other words, when you publicise and celebrate it without any good reason, you are no better than the mockers; but when you do it out of a wish to convince the one who is in the wrong and under a misapprehension about you, you are caring and beneficent.

This is exactly what David also did, not taking glory from him but anxious to root up the resentment in him. This was the reason, at any rate, that he commended him, both for his beneficence and for his mentioning his beneficence. Then, seeking a way of rewarding him but not being able to find any way equal to the deeds done, he cites to him God himself as his debtor, saying, "Because if anyone were to find his enemy in difficulties and send him on his way safe and sound, the Lord would reward him with good, as in your case today."[33] After all, what return could he have made to match the favors bestowed, even had he given him the kingdom (707) with all its cities? I mean, it was not simply cities and kingdom but even his very life that David had conferred on him, whereas he had no other life to give in return. Hence he refers him to God, and rewards him with recompense from that source, both commending him and teaching everyone that the rewards coming to us from God will be the greater when having done our enemies countless favors we receive the opposite in return.

Then he says, "See, I am aware that you will reign as king, and the kingdom of Israel will be placed in your hands. Swear to me now by the Lord that you will not destroy my offspring after me, nor wipe out my name from the house of my father."[34] How, tell me, are you aware of this? You have the armies on your side, you have the wealth, the weapons, the cities, the horses, the soldiers, all the might of kingly resources, whereas this man is alone and destitute, no city to dwell in, without hearth or home – so how, tell me, do you say this? From his very behavior, then: a man destitute, alone and unarmed would not have prevailed over such might of weaponry and equipment if he did not have God with him, whereas with God on his side he was stronger than them all. Do you see what sound values Saul had acquired after his scheming? do you see how it was possible for him to spit out all his wickedness, be changed, and return to a better condition? Let us, therefore, not be despondent about our own salvation: even if we are reduced to the depths of evil, it is possible for us to gain control of ourselves once more, become better, and set all evil aside.

What did he say next? "Swear to me by the Lord that you will not destroy my offspring after me, nor wipe out my name from the house of my father." The king presents his petition to the private citizen, and the one wearing the crown makes the request, begging the fugitive on behalf of his children. This is a sign of David's virtue, his being bold enough to ask this of an enemy. Now, if he requires an oath, it is not from lack of confidence in David's behavior but in his awareness of how much harm he had caused him. "Swear to me that you will not wipe out my offspring after me." He leaves his foe as guardian of his children and places his progeny in his hands, as if by these words taking their hands and bringing them to God as mediator. How, then, did David react? Surely he was bitterly ironical at this? Not at all: he immediately acceded and granted the favor. On the death of Saul, far from killing them on the spot, he went further than he had sworn: his offspring, who was lame and had weak legs, he brought into his own house, gave him a place at his table, and accorded him the highest honor, not ashamed of him, keeping him out of sight or considering the royal table dishonored by the child's disability; rather, he took the more pride and pleasure in it. [35]

In fact, all those who dined with him came away with a good lesson in sound values: knowing the one who enjoyed such esteem with him to be a descendant of Saul, (708) responsible for such awful harm to David, in their shame and embarrassment they made peace with their enemies, even if fiercer than any wild beast. Actually, even had he simply ordered food be provided from another source and determined an adequate system of supply, it would have been remarkable; but his also introducing him to his own table was an extraordinary example of sound values. I mean, you are well aware that it is not very easy to love enemies' children. By why say love? not to hate them, in fact, and drive them off. Many people, for example, on the death of their enemies even let loose on the children the wrath they had for them. Not so this noble man: he both looked after his enemy while alive, and on his death gave evidence to his children of his benevolence for him. What could be more sacred than his table, to which he invited the children of his foe, and a foe bent on slaughter? what could be more spiritual than that good cheer which abounded with so many blessings? It was an angel rather than a human being hosting it: embracing and loving the children of the one who made countless attempts on his life and thus ended his days put him among their ranks.

Do likewise yourselves, dearly beloved, caring for the children of your foes both when they are alive and when they die – when alive, so that by this behavior you may win over the parents, and caring for the children of the departed so as to win much favor from God, be decked in crowns beyond number, and be the object of countless prayers from everyone, not only the beneficiaries but also the onlookers. This will stand to your benefit on that day, and the enemies so indebted will be influential advocates at the time of judgement; you will expiate many of your sins and be liable for reward. Even should you have failed innumerable times, by raising that familiar prayer, "Forgive your enemies, and your Father will forgive you your falls,"[36] you will with great confidence receive forgiveness of all your sins, live here-below with sound hope, and have everyone favorably disposed to you. After all, how will those who see that you love both your foes and their children not choose to be loving and friendly, and do and put up with anything for your sake? So when you enjoy such great favor from God, and thus have everyone praying together for all good things for you, what trouble will you experience, and whose life will be more blessed than yours?

Let us not only marvel at this here: also on leaving let us take the trouble to go around and search out our enemies individually, become reconciled to them and make true friends of them. Even if there is need to excuse ourselves and beg pardon of them, do not demur, even if we are the ones who have been wronged. The reward will then be more generous, the confidence then greater, we shall then definitely attain the kingdom of heaven, thanks to the grace and lovingkindness of our Lord Jesus Christ, to whom with the Father and the Holy Spirit be glory, power and honor, now and forever, for ages of ages. Amen.

HOMILIES ON HANNAH

Unlike the homilies on David and Saul, the series that has come to be known (somewhat misleadingly) simply as *De Anna* patently acknowledges the gripping events in the life of the city of Antioch some weeks before in that year 387.[1] In opening the series on June 7, two days before the Ascension, the now more celebrated preacher recalls the events leading up to Easter Day and "the return of our father (Bishop Flavian) from his long journey" to the court in Constantinople to beg clemency for the repentant city. He also touches on the Lenten instruction he had been giving on Genesis "to the people of Antioch" (as the homilies are properly entitled, now better known as Homilies on the Statues) before having to shift his focus onto the critical situation. But the tension, palpable in the earlier series on David and Saul, is now relaxed with the happy outcome; and on a further five or six occasions up to Pentecost (at least one homily is missing) Chrysostom proceeds to speak on a variety of topics arising out of commentary on the first chapter or so of the book of 1 Samuel and loosely associated with the figure of Hannah, Samuel's mother.

It would seem that these homilies were delivered in Antioch's Old Church located in the agora, a place giving the opportunity (he suggests) for professional people to pray while waiting to enter court – and it is the efficacy of prayer that is one focus of the series. Chrysostom refers to the functions at which he is preaching in this church as συνά ξεις; which might be taken to refer simply to a paraliturgy of the Word were it not that on at least one occasion he clearly describes a eucharistic liturgy akin to Pentecost: "Where there is also reception of the blessed eucharist and sharing in other spiritual rites – I refer to things like prayer, listening, blessings, kiss of peace and all the rest, the same as today – this day will be in no respect inferior to that one, neither for you nor for me as speaker."

Why did Chrysostom choose this short section of the Former Prophets for commentary, whose author here and in the David and Saul homilies he refers to uniquely as συγγραφεύς, unlike the more elevated title προφήτης, inspired author, accorded other Old Testament composers? And why bring on stage a woman in the person of Hannah when in his commentary on other books of the Bible he has not gone out of his way to celebrate women, can let them go unnamed, and (as also occurs here) can portray them in a relatively poor light compared to their male associates? In fact, the commentary on the biblical text gets no further than chapter 2.1-2, even Hannah's prayer (2.1-10, so significant for the New Testament and in particular the Lucan Magnificat) receiving little comment, and Hannah herself fading from sight before the final homily after serving as a model for some of the preacher's chosen themes, such as formation of the young, prayer, and divine providence. It is unlikely that Chrysostom's congregation, whom he urges "not to be distracted, even by the sight of a comely woman," contained women members; he addresses them as ἄνδρες, and even if he rhetorically presents Hannah as a model for women ("You, then, woman, imitate her, and if you are childless, give evidence of this prayer") and also as a priest, ἱερεύς, superior to the priest who offered the turtledove at the presentation of young Samuel, it is unlikely that his rhetoric would translate into allowing entry of women into the presbyterate in Antioch. What he intends as a compliment to this unfortunate but brave woman comes through to us today as rather backhanded: "Though a member of the maligned and criticised sex, she repelled all the reproaches, teaching in deed the lesson that even women did not become like that by nature but by choice and their own mean-spiritedness, and that it is possible for this sex to attain the heights of virtue."

No: as in the case of the homilies on David and Saul, here too Chrysostom chooses a brief passage from the Former Prophets (in his local form of the LXX, revealing the odd peculiarity), not to respect its author's interest in the word of Lord taking effect, but for its moral and hagiographical value. As he said in his eleventh homily on Genesis, "the grace of the Spirit has left us described in the divine Scriptures both the lives of all holy people and also a pattern of life." Hannah's life as one such holy person allows him to voice concerns on married life and the education of the young; and the festal period of Pentecost prompts him to launch into further tirades against the public amusements for which the people of Antioch were notorious. The topic of drunkenness that occupied the first of the Lenten homilies reappears in the first two homilies here; and again he is incensed at the presence of some of the congregation at the racecourse after the third homily. He shows himself a shrewd observer of drunken behavior (including, it seems, the clergy's) and of contemporary morals generally; he opens his first homily by deploring young people's inadequate preparation for marriage (by comparison with Hannah's family life): "What happens these days, at any rate, is not marriage but business dealings and partying: when the young are corrupted before marriage, and after marriage still have eyes for another woman, what good is marriage, tell me?"

In berating his congregations in these homilies for their own shortcomings and the depravity of the absent, Chrysostom typically does not play the role of a spiritual guru leading them to the mystical heights of intimate union with God; Antioch was known rather for "an asceticism without mysticism," Louis Bouyer reminds us. Hannah is presented as a model of prayer, to be sure, but always prayer as a skill to be acquired: there are practical rules for it, which can be learnt (as is true of his teaching also in the Commentary on the Psalms). Her prayer sets the standard: brief, frequent prayers, not long-winded ones; the preacher recommends a mantra for praying at work, "Have mercy on me, O God." Hannah is also a model of that favorite Antiochene virtue, enthusiasm, personal effort, προθυμία (its correlative ῥᾳθυμία, indifference); Luther's scorn for Chrysostom would be fostered by hearing him commend his heroine for winning divine grace (in the form of Samuel) through prayer, since "it is not only through faith but also through works" that we make confession in God. The gratuity of divine grace is not so readily conceded.

While we today are fascinated in reading these homilies "On Hannah" for aspects of them such as the rare focus on a woman from Old Testament times and the inventory of vices and virtues in contemporary Antioch, we also wonder why – to judge from the text – so many of the congregation soon absented themselves from the συνάξεις to attend amusement such as the races. Perhaps it was the homilist's notorious *makrologia*, which only for some brought a bare scriptural text to life with flowing Homeric similes; perhaps it was the disappointment of others, who felt the homilist had forsaken his promise to comment on the biblical text to rehearse once again the familiar catalogue of their shortcomings; perhaps it was the always galling experience of being upbraided for the absence of others; perhaps it was the novel experience of having a woman paraded (at least for a time) as a model of prayerfulness and education of the young. In our days we find these accents valuable in addition to the light the homilies cast on the dark days of that Lent of 387 and the aftermath, and we appreciate them also as documenting further our knowledge of theological, hermeneutical, and spiritual principles honored in Antioch.

Homily One

On the need to remember fasting at Pentecost and at all times, [1]
and the fact that not only the presence but also the memory of
fasting is of benefit.
Also on God's providence and the fact that, besides other things,
no small part of it is the natural love of parents for their offspring,
and the fact that it is required not only of fathers but also of
mothers to control their children.
And, towards the end, about Hannah.

When we have given a warm welcome to some guest who lodges with us for a few days, we share with them conversation and repast and send them on their way. On the day after their departure, however, on laying the table we immediately recall them and the exchange of ideas, and with great love we miss them. Let us do exactly this in the case of fasting as well: it lodged with us for forty days, we gave it a warm welcome and sent it on its way. [2] So now that we are on the point of laying a spiritual table, let us recall it and all the good things that came to us from it. I mean, it is not only the presence of fasting but also the memory of fasting that can be of the greatest benefit. Just as our loved ones fill us with deep satisfaction not only when they are present but also when they come to mind, so too the fast days, the assemblies, the time spent together and all the other good things we gained from it give joy to us on recalling them, and if we bring them to mind and remember them, (633) we shall gain a great deal even at the present time. [3]

I say this, not to oblige you to fast, but to persuade you not to give way to luxurious living nor behave like most human beings – if in fact one ought to give the name human beings to those living in such a mean-spirited way, who like people released from their bonds and freed from some harsh prison say to one another, We have finally come to the end of the awful ocean of fasting. Others with less gumption than these are even in dread of the Lent to come. This comes about from giving themselves up to luxurious living all the remaining time, to prodigality and drunkenness. If on the contrary we too care to live a steady and modest life all the other days of the year, we would long for fasting when it had gone, and with deep satisfaction would welcome it when it was due to come around.

After all, what good does not come to us from fasting? It is productive of complete tranquillity and pure calm. Are not even households freed from alarm and excursions and all kinds of tumult? But ahead of households the mind of those fasting enjoys this repose; and the whole city reproduces the good order in the mind and in the houses. That is, at evening time you are not treated to loud sounds, nor in the day to the noise of rioters and revelers, no shouting or brawling – instead, you can see complete peace everywhere. It is not like this today, however: right from the crack of dawn there is shouting and rioting, cooks racing hither and yon, houses full of smoke, minds full of smoke, passions afire within us, the flame of lust for indecent things aroused by luxurious living. [4]

This is the reason we miss fasting even when it is gone: it keeps all this in check. Even if we lay aside its demands, let us not suppress yearning for it nor extinguish memory of it. Instead, when we have had lunch and a rest, and venture forth, let us on seeing the day fading towards evening come into this church, approach this altar and recall the time of fasting when the church was filled with the congregation, there was intense enthusiasm for listening, there was deep satisfaction and everyone's mind was aroused. Calling all this to mind, recall those days we long for. If you are on the point of laying the table, take the food while remembering this, and you will never be in a position to fall into drunkenness;

instead, just as a man with a wife who is steady, self-controlled and a free spirit, with whom he is on fire with love, would not even in her absence be attracted to an immoral and corrupt woman, desire for his wife preoccupying his mind and not allowing a different love to gain entrance, just so is it the case both with fasting and with drunkenness. If, then, we were to remember the free and self-controlled woman, on the one hand, we would on the other elude with great ease the common prostitute, mother of all indecency – I refer to drunkenness – the desire for fasting repelling her shamelessness more sharply than any hand.[5] (634)

For all these very reasons, I beseech you, let us always keep those days in mind. Now, for the purpose of my contributing something to that recollection, I shall try to develop now as well the same theme I tried to outline then so that some memory of that time might come to you also through the similarity as far as content is concerned. I mean, you may have forgotten, owing to our many addresses being delivered in the meantime, not to mention other things as well:[6] with our father's return from his long journey it was necessary to tell everything that had happened in regard to the palace, and after that to engage the pagans in lengthy discourse so that they might become better from the disaster, leave pagan error and come over to us, and we might give them secure root and teach them the kind of darkness they have been freed from and the nature of the light of truth to which they have had recourse. After that we enjoyed in turn for many days the festival of the martyrs, and it would have been improper for us, while spending time at the tombs of the martyrs, to take our leave without sharing in the tributes due to the martyrs. To these tributes succeeded in turn the exhortation about the oaths: since we had witnessed the invasion of all the country folk into the city, we wanted, after giving them this sustenance for the journey, to send them all away from us so equipped.

For this reason, then, while it would not be reasonably possible for us to report to you the discussion held by us at that time with the pagans, I shall find it within me, being constantly involved in these things and bearing this responsibility, and having mentioned the highlights of what was said on that occasion, to recall the whole theme of the discourse. [7] So what was our theme? We studied the question as to how from the beginning God showed providence for our race, and how he gave us useful lessons, without there being any writing or any gift of the Scriptures; and we brought out the fact that he guided us to knowledge of him through discernment of creation. [8]

At that time, without taking you by the hand and instead appealing to your mind, we made a survey of the whole of creation, highlighting heaven, earth, sea, lakes, springs, rivers, mighty oceans, meadows, gardens, flowering crops, trees laden with fruit, and mountain peaks covered with timber. At that time I had much to say also about seeds, grasses, flowers, plants that bear fruit and those that do not, beasts gentle and wild, on sea and on land and amphibious creatures, those that fly through the air and those that crawl on the ground, and about the very elements of everything. We all together cried aloud at each marvel, our mind struck by the immeasurable wealth and incapable of grasping it all, "How your works are magnified, O Lord! You made everything in wisdom." [9] We marveled at God's wisdom, not only for the number of works but also for both these features, that the creation he made is beautiful, mighty and wonderful, and that in turn he implanted in visible things many signs of its limitations [10] – the former for him to be admired for his wisdom and to draw the witnesses to worship of him, and the latter in case those perceiving their beauty and might should pass over their maker (635) and adore the visible things instead of him, the limitations within them being capable of such an awful error.

How the whole of creation is corruptible, will be transformed to a better condition and will enjoy greater glory, when and why and for what reason it happened – all this we brought out in argument for your benefit. From this we showed God's power, that in corruptible bodies he produced such wonderful beauty, which God had allotted them even from the beginning – that of the stars, of heaven, of the sun. It is, in fact, really remarkable how despite the passing of the years they suffered none of the change our bodies do, nor did they grow weaker with age, nor were they debilitated by disease or illness, and instead they continue to maintain their peculiar bloom and beauty which, as I said before, God had allotted them. The sun's light was not worn out, nor did the brightness of the stars become dimmer, the clarity of heaven did not ebb away, the boundaries of the sea were not moved, the ability of the earth to produce its annual fruits was not extinguished. While the fact that these things are corruptible we demonstrated both from reason and from the divine Scriptures, the fact that they are good and splendid and have retained their bloom undiminished the daily experience of viewers confirms, which is something to be particularly admired on the part of the one who created them this way from the beginning.

Since, however, at the time we were saying this some people objected by claiming, it follows that the human being is of lower standing than all these visible things if it is true that the body of heaven, and of earth, and of sun, and the life of all the stars has gone on for such a long time, whereas mortals disappear after seventy years and perish, I would reply this way. Firstly, the whole living being does not disappear: its more characteristic and more basic element, the soul, abides forever immortal, not subject to any of the passions, and corruption affects the lesser part. Second, we are shown greater esteem even for this very reason: it is not by chance or without any reason, but justly and to our good that we suffer old age and disease – justly in that we fell into sin, and to our good so that the arrogance innate in us from indifference we may correct through this deficiency and the passions. [11]

So it was not to accord us lower standing that God allowed this to happen: if he had accorded us lower standing, he would not have let our soul be immortal. Nor was it out of weakness that he made our body this way: were he weak, he could not have ensured that heaven, the stars and the body of earth would retain their force for such a long time; rather, it was to make us better, more temperate and more compliant to him, which is the basis of complete salvation. This was why he made heaven not subject to the decay of old age in time or to other such infirmities: the person bereft of free will could likewise neither commit sin nor do right, and hence would have no need of such correction. In our case, on the other hand, endowed as we are with reason and soul, the self-control and humility coming from these passions were necessary since even at the beginning, the human being made first went to the excess of folly before all the others. Otherwise, if heaven had been intended to be formed like our bodies and grow old, many people would have charged the (636) maker with great weakness as being incapable of keeping one body in existence for a long period of years, whereas in fact even the very pretext has been removed from them, since the works continue in existence for so long. [12]

Even beyond what has been said, however, our condition will not remain at this point; rather, after we have been properly chastened in the present life, our bodies will arise with greater glory and will be more resplendent than heaven, sun and all other things, and they will be transformed into the better state on high. So one way to knowledge of God is through the whole of creation; another, not inferior, is the way of conscience, which we on that occasion developed at great length, showing how the knowledge of things that are good and things that are not is acquired by us automatically, and how conscience inspires us with this interiorly. [13] These two, in fact, have been our teachers from the beginning – creation and conscience: without either of them uttering a word, they taught human beings in silence, creation making an impression on the observer through vision and leading the observer of everything to the marvel of its maker, conscience inspiring us within and suggesting all that has to be done, so that through the visible aspect we grasp his power and the verdict he delivers. That is to say, whenever it accuses sin on the inside, it suffuses the countenance outside, and fills us with deep regret. Again, it renders us pale and timid when we are caught in something shameful; and while we do not hear a word, we perceive the irritation happening within from the external aspect.

Along with these two, however, the sermon showed you also a third teacher given in addition by the providence of God, no longer voiceless like the former ones; instead, by word, exhortation and advice it controls our free will. What is this? The parents assigned to each of us: God caused us to be loved by our parents for this reason, that we might have mentors in virtue. [14] You see, he does not make fathers only for having children but also for instructing them properly, nor cause mothers to give birth to children but also to nourish them properly. The truth of this, that it is not nature but virtue that makes parents, the parents themselves would admit to us. At any rate, it often happens that when they see them go bad and give way to evil impulses, they expel them from their kinship and disinherit them, taking as their children others that are often in no way related to them. What could be more baffling than that, to reject those they gave birth to and replace them with those they did not give birth to?

It was not without purpose that we told you this; rather, it was for you to learn that free will is more influential than nature, and that it is the former rather than the latter that normally constitutes both children and parents. This was an effect of God's providence, not to leave children bereft of natural affection, nor in turn to entrust everything to it. After all, if parents were in no way moved by natural inclination to love their children, but only by morality (637) and virtuous behavior, you would see many expelled from the family home on account of their own indifference and our human race thrown into disorder. Again, if he had entrusted everything to the tyranny of nature, and did not allow us to hate those that are evil, and instead parents were maltreated by them and subjected to countless abuses, and through force of nature they continued to shower attention on the children who abused them and were guilty of drunken behavior, our race would be reduced to the extremes of misfortune. I mean, if these days there are children who, though not having complete confidence in nature but aware that many who turn bad are rejected from their parents' home and possessions, nevertheless in many cases count on the affection of parents and maltreat those who brought them into the world, what end would there be to wickedness had not God allowed parents to be angry, take action against the children that have become evil, and reject them. Hence, both by force of nature and by the behavior of children God instilled affection in parents so that they might both give reasonable pardon to children who err, nature urging them to it, and also refrain from encouraging those that have gone bad and are in the grip of incurable ailments to go from bad to worse, in cases where nature is once more reproachful and capable of pressuring them into fawning upon children, even those gone bad.

How great a mark of providence is this, tell me, both the command to love and the imposition of a norm for affection, and as well the provision for a reward for good upbringing? I mean, for proof that a reward is available, not only for husbands but also for wives, listen to how Scripture in many places addresses even the latter about these things, and no less the latter than the husbands. Paul, remember, after saying, "The woman was deceived and became the transgressor," went on, "But she will be saved through childbearing." [15] Now, what he means is something like this: Are you disappointed that the first woman committed you to the pangs and labor of childbirth and a long period of gestation? Do not be troubled: you are not subjected to hardship from birth-pangs and labor to the extent of the gain you receive, if you so wish, in making the rearing of children an occasion of virtuous actions. I mean, the children being born, provided they receive proper care and are brought up to virtue by your attention, prove a basis and occasion of complete salvation for you; and in addition to your own virtuous acts you will receive a great reward for your care of them.

For you to learn that it is not the bearing of children that makes a mother, and that the reward does not come from that, Paul spoke in similar terms elsewhere in talking of a widow, "If she raised children." [16] He did not say, If she bore children, but "If she raised children:" one thing comes from nature, the other from free will. Hence in saying here as well, "She will be saved through child-bearing," he did not stop at that point, but in his wish to bring out that it is not bearing children but raising children well that brings us this reward, he went on, "If they continue in faith, in love and in holiness along with self-control." What he means is this: You will then receive a great reward if those begetting the children continue in faith, in love, and in holiness. So if you bring them up to these things, if you encourage them, if you teach them, if you advise (638) them, a great reward for this care will be laid up for you with God. Let not the women, therefore, consider it beyond them to care for both the girls and the boys. Gender made no difference in these instances, note: he simply said in the one case, "If she raised children," and in the other, "If they continue in faith, in love, and in holiness." And so care is to be taken by us of both lots of children, and especially by the women, to the extent that they also stay at home more. After all, traveling, public affairs and business in town often fall to the husbands, whereas the wife enjoys exemption from all such concerns and would be in a position to look after the infants more easily, enjoying much free time as she does.

That is what women in olden times did: this commitment was required not only of husbands but also of wives – I mean the care of their children and their education. For proof that this is true, I shall recount to you the ancient record. Hannah was a woman of the Jews. This Hannah had worried about childlessness for a long time, and to make it worse, her rival was the mother of many children. [17] Now, you realise that by nature and in itself this is an intolerable situation for a woman; but when a rival comes on the scene with children, it becomes far worse. I mean, from that woman's good luck she gets a keener sense of her own misfortune, just as those living in extreme poverty suffer more when they come across those who are wealthy. The fact that she had no children while the other woman did was not the only problem: there was also the fact that this woman was her rival – and not simply that she was her rival but that she provoked her out of scorn for her. [18] Though God saw all this, he did not intervene; Scripture says, "The Lord did not give her a child in her tribulation and in her depression of soul." [19] What is meant by "in her tribulation"? You cannot say, the text means, that on seeing her meekly bearing this calamity he prevented her giving birth; rather, although seeing her distraught, pained, distressed, he did not remove her depression, planning as he was something far more significant.

Let us not take this with a grain of salt; instead, let us learn also from this the highest values, and when we fall foul of some disaster, even if we are suffering grief and pain, even if the trouble seems insupportable to us, let us not be anxious or beside ourselves, but wait on God's providence. He is well aware, after all, when is the time for what is causing us depression to be removed – which is what happened in her case as well. It was not out of hatred, in fact, nor of revulsion that he closed her womb, but to open to us the doors on the values the woman possessed, and for us to espy the riches of her faith and realise that he rendered her more conspicuous on that account. Listen also to what follows: "He acted this way year after year for a long time," Scripture says, "as she went up to the house of the Lord. She was dispirited, she wept and would not eat." [20] Extreme the pain, great the (639) length of the grief – not two or three days, not twenty or a hundred, not a thousand or twice as much; instead, "for a long time," it says, for many years the woman was grieving and distressed, the meaning of "for a long time." Yet she showed no impatience, nor did the length of time undermine her values, nor the reproaches and abuse of her rival; instead, she was unremitting in prayer and supplication, and what was most remarkable of all, showing in particular her love for God, was the fact that she was not simply anxious to have this very child for herself, but to dedicate the fruit of her womb to God, offer the first fruits of her own womb, and receive the reward for this fine promise.

How does this emerge? From the following verses. I mean, you all doubtless understand that childlessness is intolerable to wives particularly for their husbands' sake: many people are so unreasonable in their attitude as to rebuke their wives when they do not have children, not realising that having children has its origins on high, in God's providence, and it is not the nature of a wife or sexual intercourse or anything else that is solely responsible for it. Yet even though they at least accept that they are wrong to rebuke them, they often reproach and reject them, and find no satisfaction in relating to them. [21] So let us see if this happened also in this woman's case. That is to say, if you were to see her despised, dishonored, abused, lacking confidence in her husband, and enjoying no great regard, you would be able to guess that she longed for a child for this reason, to have great confidence and freedom, and prove more desirable to her husband. But if you were to find things quite the opposite, that she was loved more than the woman with children, and was the recipient of greater regard, it is clear that she was longing for a child for no human reason, to be more appealing to her husband, but for the reason mentioned.

How is this obvious, then? Listen to the historian in person saying so; [22] it was not without purpose that he mentioned it, but for you to learn the woman's virtue. So what does he say? "In fact, Elkanah loved Hannah more than Peninnah." Then, after later seeing her not eating but crying, he said, "What are you crying about? Why are you not eating? Why does your heart grieve? Am I not more to you than ten sons?" [23] Do you see how he was attached to her, and was upset more for her sake, not for her not having children but from seeing her dejected and in the grip of distress? Yet he failed to persuade her to recover from her depression: she wanted the child not for him but so as to give evidence of some fruitfulness to God. "She arose," the text says, "after they had eaten at Shiloh and after drinking, and took her place before the Lord." [24] It was not without purpose that it did not simply say, [25] After eating and drinking: it was for us to learn that the time which others give to rest and repose she gave to prayer and tears for the purpose of strict vigil and watching.

"She took her place before the Lord. Eli the priest," the text goes on, "was sitting on the seat by the doorposts of the Temple of the Lord." It was not without purpose that it said, "Eli the priest was sitting by the doorposts of the Temple of the Lord," but to bring out the woman's fervor. You see, just as a widow who is destitute and all alone, much (640) abused and wronged, will often not be alarmed at the imminent triumphal procession of emperor, bodyguards, shield-bearers, horses, and all the rest of his advance retinue, but without need of a patron will brush past them all and with great confidence accost the emperor, exaggerating her own situation under pressure of her sense of need, so too this woman was not embarrassed, was not ashamed, though the priest was sitting there, to make her request in person and with great confidence approach the king. Instead, under the impulse of desire and in her mind ascending to heaven as though she saw God himself, she addressed him this way with complete ardor. What did she say? Instead of saying anything at first, she began with wailing, and shed warm floods of tears. And just as, when rains storms fall, even the harder ground is moistened and softened, and easily bestirs itself to produce crops, so too did this happen in the case of this woman: as though softened by the flood of tears and warmed with the pangs, the womb began to stir in that wonderful fertility. [26]

Let us listen also to the words themselves and this beautiful supplication. "She wept and lamented, and directed her prayer to the Lord in the words, Adonai Kyrie Elohi Sabaoth." [27] Fearsome words, fit to terrify. The historian was right not to translate them into our language: his ability did not suffice to turn them into the Greek tongue. Instead of invoking him in a single word, the woman betrayed her love for him and her ardent feelings with many titles of his. Just as those writing their appeals to the emperor do not apply a single epithet but include Victorious, August, Imperial and many others more sublime than these, and thus make their supplication, so too this woman in offering an appeal to God used many names in beginning her appeal, both betraying her own affection, as I said before, and the respect for the person addressed. Pain prompted the appeal itself; hence the one composing it with great shrewdness was quickly heard.

This is what prayers arising from the soul's pangs are like: her mind took the place of paper, her tongue a pen, and her tears ink;[28] hence her appeal has lasted to this very day. Such letters, in fact, prove indelible, dipped as they are in that ink.

While the beginning of her appeal was of that kind, what was the rest like? "If you will really look upon the lowliness of your handmaid," she says. Without yet receiving anything, she began her prayer with a promise. She already repays God without having anything in her hand. She was more concerned about one condition rather than the other, and on its account she prayed to have the child: "If you will really look upon the lowliness of your handmaid." I have two claims, she is saying, servitude and calamity. "Give me, your handmaid, a male child; I will give him as a gift before you." What is the meaning of "a gift before you"? (641) As a present and a complete slave; I forfeit all ownership. In fact, I am anxious to become a mother to such an extent that the child takes its beginning from me, and then I withdraw and hand him over.

Take note of the woman's reverence: she did not say, If you give me three, I shall give you two; or if two, I shall give you one. Instead, If you give me one, I shall dedicate the offspring wholly to you. "He will not drink wine or strong drink." She had not yet received the child, and was already forming a prophet, talking about his upbringing and making a deal with God. What wonderful confidence on a woman's part! Since she could not make a deposit on account of not having anything, she pays the price from what is coming to her. Just as many farmers who are living in extreme poverty, but have no money to buy a calf or sheep, get them on credit from their masters by pledging to pay the price from the crops that are due, just so did she do, too – or rather much more: she did not take her son from God on credit but on condition of returning him wholly to him once again and reaping the fruit of his upbringing. She regarded it as sufficient reward, you see, to devote her labors to God's priest.

"He will not drink wine or strong drink," it says. She did not entertain within herself the thoughts, What effect will the drinking of water have on him when he is of tender years? What if he falls ill? What if he dies, falling victim to some severe illness? Instead, considering that the one who gave him would be able personally to provide for good health, she set him on course for holiness from the very cradle and birth, casting everything onto God; her womb containing a prophet, bearing a priest and carrying an offering, a living offering, was sanctified before birth. For this reason God yielded to her disappointment, hence he finally granted her request so as to make her more famous by the manner of the birth in order to bring out her sound values: in taking her position at prayer she did not call to mind her rival, she did not mention her abuse, she did not expose her reproaches, she did not say, Take vengeance for me on that loathsome and wicked woman, as do many women. [29] Instead, without even recalling those reproaches, she prayed only in regard to what had befallen her.

Do likewise yourself, mortal that you are, [30] and when you see your foe experiencing sorrow, direct no harsh word to him, nor pray to his detriment for being hostile to you; rather, go in to him, bend your knee, shed tears, exhort God to relieve his depression, to extinguish his grief – which is what she in fact did, and from the woman who was her enemy she reaped the highest benefit, the woman actually assisting in the birth of the child. How this happened, I shall tell you. Because she reproached her, distressed her and caused her even greater pain, her prayer was made more assiduous by her suffering, the prayer won God over and secured his acquiescence, and thus Samuel was born. And so, if we are vigilant, not only will enemies be unable to harm us, but they will even bring us the greatest benefit, making us more zealous for every cause, provided we bring ourselves to utter not abuse and insults but prayers (642) as a result of the discouragement caused us by them.

After giving birth to the child, she called him Samuel,[31] that is, He will hear God: since she got him from being heard and from praying and not from nature, she wanted the memory of the doing to be imposed as a name of the child for the future, as though on some bronze pillar. She did not say, Let us give him his father's name, or his uncle's, or his grandfather's, or his great-grandfather's; instead she said, Let the one who has given him be the one also honored by the child's name. Women, emulate her; men, imitate her, and let us show similar care for our children, let us bring up our offspring in similar fashion, in every matter and especially in that of self-control. Nothing, in fact, should be so much the object of our care and concern for young people as self-control and seriousness: it is an area that is a particular problem for people of that age.

What we do with lamps we should be careful about with the young, too; we often give instructions, remember, to the maidservant handling a lamp not to take a lamp where there is hay or straw or anything like that in case, unbeknown to us, a spark falls and takes hold of that material and sets fire to the whole house. Let us take this precaution with the young people, too, and not draw their attention to where there are loose housemaids, immodest damsels, licentious slave girls; instead, let us give instructions and advice if we have such a housemaid or such a neighbor or anyone else of that kind not to enter into conversation with the young lest a spark fall from it and engulf the soul of the youngster, and the calamity prove irreparable.[32] It is not only spectacles but also effeminate and undisciplined sounds that we should keep them from lest their soul be beguiled by them; nor should we take them to theatres, banquets or parties. Rather, young people should be protected by us more than closeted virgins, nothing being so calculated to adorn that age as the wreath of self-control and coming to marriage devoid of all intemperance. Likewise women, too, would be more desirable to them when the soul has had no previous experience of fornication or has been corrupted, when the young person is acquainted only with that woman who is joined to him in marriage. Likewise lovers are more ardent, favor more genuine and affection more fervent when the young approach marriage with caution of this kind.

What happens these days,[33] at any rate, is not marriage but business dealings and partying: when the young are corrupted even before marriage, and after marriage still have eyes for another woman, what good is marriage, tell me? So the punishment is greater, the sin unpardonable, when despite his wife living with him he is unfaithful to her and commits adultery. I mean, after marriage, even if the one who corrupts the married man is a prostitute,[34] it is a case of adultery. Now, this happens, (643) and they betake themselves to women who are whores, because they did not practise self-control before marriage. This is the source of fights, abuse, broken homes and daily squabbles; this is the source of the love for one's wife waning and dying, since association with the prostitutes puts an end to it. But if he learns to practise self-control, he will consider his wife more desirable than anyone, will look upon her with great favor, maintain harmony with her, and where there is peace and harmony, all good things will come to that house.

In order, then, that things in this life also be managed well, and after them we attain also the kingdom of heaven, let us look after our own children for the sake of the commandment in particular, lest we enter those spiritual nuptials clad in soiled garments instead of enjoying with great confidence the dignity available there to the deserving. May it be the good fortune of us all to attain this, thanks to the grace and lovingkindness of our Lord Jesus Christ, to whom with the Father and the Holy Spirit be glory, honor and might, now and forever, for ages of ages. Amen.

Homily Two

*On the faith of Hannah, and on her sound values and goodness,
and to do with respect for the priests,
and on the need to pray at the beginning and end of lunch.*

Nothing, then, matches prayer, dearly beloved, nothing is more efficacious than faith. Just the other day Hannah exemplified both for us:[1] approaching God with these gifts, she achieved all she wanted, set to rights her natural deficiency, opened her closed womb, took away her shame, dismissed the taunts of her rival, and restored herself to great confidence, reaping a bumper crop from barren rock. You all heard how she prayed, how she begged, pleaded and received her request, conceived, bore and made an offering of Samuel. And so anyone would not be wide of the mark in calling this woman the child's mother and father at the same time: even if the husband sowed the seed, her prayer supplied the potency to the seed and rendered the beginnings of Samuel's birth more august. After all, it was really not only the parents' sleeping together and having intercourse, as in other cases; rather, prayers, tears and faith formed the beginnings of this birth, and the prophet had more august parents than other children, having come into being as a result of his mother's faith. Hence of this woman, too, you could appositely say, "Though sowing in tears, they will reap in joy."[2]

Let the men among us emulate her, let the women among us imitate her: the woman is teacher of both sexes. Those who are sterile, let them not despair; those who are mothers, let them bring up in this fashion the children they have borne; and let everyone emulate this woman's faith in giving birth and zeal following the birth. I mean, what could reveal sounder values than the way she meekly and nobly put up in such a manner with an intolerable calamity, and did not desist until she had escaped the disaster and discovered a remarkable and baffling outcome of the problem, finding no helper or ally here-below. In fact, she experienced the Lord's lovingkindness – hence she made her approach on her own, and achieved what she wanted. That is to say, (644) the remedy for that depression depended not on human help but on divine grace; it lay not in expenditure of money by which a person settles the depression by laying out cash, nor in bodily weakness by which you summon medical colleagues and drive off the ailment. It was nature that was out of sorts, requiring intervention from on high – hence she passed over everything on earth and had recourse to the Lord of nature, nor did she desist until she had persuaded him to cancel her childlessness, open her womb and make the sterile woman a mother.

Blessed is she, therefore, even on this account, not for being a mother, but for becoming one after not being one: while the former is a common attribute of nature, the latter was the woman's commendable achievement. While she is blessed, therefore, even for those pangs, she is no less blessed also on account of everything before the pangs. I mean, you are all assuredly aware, women and men both, that nothing could be more intolerable for a woman than childlessness; even if she experienced satisfaction in countless other ways, she would never be rid of the pain coming to her from this affliction. Yet if it is so intolerable these days when we are called to much higher values and are on our way to heaven, when no thought for present realities affects us, and instead we are preparing ourselves for a different life and the esteem for virginity is high, think of how great an affliction the matter was considered in those days when there was not the slightest hope of a future nor any conception of it by people of olden times, and instead they did everything with an eye to present realities, and being barren and childless was a sort of curse and death sentence. It is impossible to describe or present in words the pain of this affliction. Witnesses to it are all those women who, though giving evidence of high-mindedness in everything else, could not bear the opprobrium of this; instead, some became a nuisance to their husbands, while others regarded their life as unlivable.

What was besetting this woman, however, was not only depression as a result of barrenness but also a different feeling, anger at the taunts of her rival. Just as, when contrary winds blow against one another and catch a boat up in the midst of the strife, stirring up waves, some at the stern, some at the bow, the steersman seated at the tiller saves the boat by avoiding the onset of the waves through the skill of his trade, so too that woman at that time, when anger and depression beset her soul like contrary winds, disturbing her thoughts and stirring up many waves, not for two or three or twenty days but for whole years (it went on for a long time, Scripture says, remember),[3] survived the tempest nobly and did not allow her thoughts to go under. The fear of God, in fact, like a steersman seated at the tiller, persuaded her to see out the billows in noble fashion, and did not cease steering her soul until he brought to the safe haven the vessel loaded with cargo, the womb bearing its precious treasure. She was carrying, of course, not gold or silver, but a prophet and priest; (645) the sanctification of her womb was twofold, being pregnant with such a child, and receiving the beginning of pregnancy both from prayer and from grace above.[4] Now, it was not only that the cargo was baffling and remarkable: the manner of commerce proved even more baffling. I mean, she did not sell it to people, neither to merchants nor to pedlars; instead, once she unloaded it from the vessel she offered it for sale to God, and she made as great a profit as was fitting for her to make as one who had dealings with God.[5] After God had accepted him, remember, he repaid her with another child – or, rather, not one, or two, or three, or four only, but even many more: Scripture says, "The barren woman bore seven children,"[6] and the interest surpassed the principal. Dealings with God are like that, you see: far from giving a small return on the principal, he makes a return many times the amount. Instead of giving her only girls,[7] he made her offspring a blend of both sexes so that her joy would be complete.

I tell you this not only for you to praise her but also for you to emulate the woman's faith and longsuffering, of which you heard partly the other day. But for the sake of filling in the remainder, allow me to speak briefly on the words spoken to the priest and the priest's boy after the first prayer so that you may come to know the woman's gentle and mild attitude. "It happened," the text goes on, "that when she continued praying before the Lord, Eli the priest observed her mouth."[8] Here the historian testifies to the twofold virtue of the woman, her persistence in prayer and the alertness of her mind, the former by saying "she continued" and the latter by the addition of "before the Lord." I mean, while we all pray, we do not all do it before the Lord: when the body is lying on the ground and the mouth is babbling on, and the mind wandering through all parts of the house and the market place, how will such people be in a position to claim that they prayed before the Lord?[9] In fact, they pray before the Lord who summon their soul away from all distractions and have nothing in common with the earth, but transport themselves to heaven and expel all human thinking from their soul. Just so did this woman, then, on that occasion: she recollected herself completely and concentrated her thinking, and thus called upon God with her soul in pain.

But how is it that the text says that "she continued" her prayer? Surely the woman's length of prayer was short, for one thing: she did not reach to drawn-out expressions nor extend her supplication to great length; rather, the words she uttered were short and sweet. "Adonai Kyrie Elohi Sabaoth, if you will only look upon the lowliness of your handmaid and remember me, not forget your handmaid and give your handmaid a male child, I shall give him as a gift before you till the day of his death. He will not drink wine or strong drink, (646) and iron will not reach his head." [10] What sort of lengthy words are these? So why did he suggest it in saying, "She continued"? She kept saying the same thing over and over again, and did not stop spending a long time with the same words. This, at any rate, is the way Christ bade us pray in the Gospels: telling the disciples not to pray like the pagans and use a lot of words, [11] he taught us moderation in prayer to bring out that being heard comes not from the number of words but from the alertness of mind. So how is it, you ask, that if our prayers must be brief, he told them a parable on the need to pray always, namely, the one about the widow who by the constancy of her request wore down the cruel and inhumane judge, who had fear neither of God nor of men, by the persistence of her appeal? [12] And how is it that Paul exhorts us in the words, "Persevere in prayer," and again, "Pray without ceasing"? [13] I mean, if we must not reach to lengthy statements, and must pray constantly, one command is at variance with the other.

It is not at variance, however – perish the thought; it is quite consistent: both Christ and Paul bade us make brief and frequent prayers at short intervals. You see, if you extend your prayers to great length without paying much attention in many cases, you would provide the devil with great security in making his approach, tripping you up and distracting your thoughts from what you are saying. If, on the other hand, you are in the habit of making frequent prayers, dividing all your time into brief intervals with your frequency, you would easily be able to keep control of yourself and recite the prayers themselves with great attention. [14] This, in fact, is what she also did, not reaching to long-winded expressions, but unceasingly making her approach to God at frequent intervals. Then, when the priest put a stop to her praying – the meaning of the verse, "He observed her mouth: her lips moved but her voice was not audible" – she was forced to obey the priest and stop praying. So her voice was stopped, but there was no stopping her confidence: her heart cried out inside all the more fervently. This is what prayer is most of all, you see, when the cries are raised inside; this is the particular mark of a distressed soul, giving evidence of prayer not in volume but in ardor of mind. This was the way Moses prayed, too; hence, though he actually uttered no word, God said, "Why are you calling out to me?" [15] I mean, human beings hearken only to this voice of ours, whereas God hears those crying out on the inside ahead of it. So it is possible for those not calling out to be heard, for those walking in the market place to pray in the mind with great assiduity, and for those meeting with friends and doing any old thing to call on God with an ardent cry – inside, I mean – and to do so without it being obvious to anyone present.

So that is what this woman did on that occasion: "Her voice was not heard," Scripture says, and God hearkened to her. "Eli's boy said to her, 'How long will you be drunk? Rid yourself of your wine, and leave the presence of the Lord.'" [16] Here in particular you can see the woman's sound values. At home her rival mocked her; she went into the temple, and the priest's boy abused her and the priest (647) upbraided her. She fled the storm at home, entered port and still ran into turbulence; she went to get a remedy, and not only did not get it but received an additional burden of taunts, and the wound instead was opened up again. You are aware, of course, how distressed souls are susceptible to abuse and insult: just as bad wounds cannot stand the slightest contact with the hand but become worse, so too the soul that is disturbed and upset has problems with everything and is stung by a chance remark. The woman, on the contrary, was not like that, even in this case with the boy abusing her. Had the priest been intoxicated, the insults would not have been so surprising; his high rank and heavy responsibility convinced her against her will to keep her composure. But in fact she was not even upset with the priest's boy, and hence she won God's favor even further. Should we too be abused and suffer countless misadventures, let us put up nobly with those who insult us, and we shall thus win greater favor from God.

How does this become obvious? From what happened to David. What, in fact, did he have to put up with? He was on one occasion exiled from his country, his freedom and very life were at risk, the army switched its loyalties to that intemperate young man, tyrant and parricide as he was, he wandered in the wilderness, and yet he did not get upset or complain to God, nor did he say, Why is this happening? did he allow son to rebel against father? even if admittedly he had just cause for complaint, it should not have happened this way; as it is, without being wronged by us in small matter or great, he goes about with the desire to stain his hand with his father's blood, and God sees it and lets it happen. He said none of these things, however. And what is even more remarkable, when he was wandering about and rejected by everyone, a wicked and deranged fellow called Shimei assailed him, labeling him a murderer and profaner, and heaping countless other insults on him. [17] But if someone were to object, To be sure, why is it remarkable if in his weakened condition he did not take vengeance, lacking the means? I should reply, first, I would not be so much surprised if when in possession of crown and kingdom and seated on his throne he then put up with being abused as I am now filled with praise and amazement at his display of sound values in the time of disaster; then it was that his burden of responsibility and the lowly condition of the one abusing him persuaded him on many occasions to treat it with contempt. Many other kings, too, many times reached that conclusion, taking the excessive frenzy of the ones hurling abuse as the basis for so acting. After all, in our case likewise when we are maltreated while enjoying prosperity, insults naturally get to us; but when we are down, then it is they affect us more keenly and sting us more sharply. In his case, by contrast, there is nothing more to add to what has been said, that he was in a position to take vengeance but did not (648) take vengeance. For you to learn that his sound values were a mark not of weakness but of longsuffering, when the commander at that time wanted permission to go over and have the man's head, David not only gave no permission but was even upset, saying, "What difference does it make to me or to you, son of Zeruiah? Let him curse me so that the Lord may see my humility and grant me good things in place of this curse of his today" [18] – which is what happened.

Do you see how the righteous man recognised that nobly bearing insults proves a basis for greater approval? Hence on one occasion he had Saul within his grasp within a double wall and was in a position to kill him but he spared his life, and this despite the fact those present were urging him to use his sword. [19] But neither the ease of the opportunity, nor the prompting of the others, nor his suffering many injustices, nor the likelihood of suffering worse ones allowed him to draw his sword, even though guilt for this murder would not be likely to be betrayed to the army; it was a cave, you see, and there was no one besides himself present. He did not say, as someone committing adultery said, "Darkness and walls surround me: what should I worry about?" [20] Instead, he had the unsleeping eye before him, and he knew that the eyes of the Lord are infinitely brighter than the sun. Hence he did and said everything just as if he were present and making a judgement on his words; so he said, "I shall not lay a hand on the Lord's anointed." [21] I do not see his wickedness: I see his position instead. Let no one tell me that he is a man of violence and blood: I am afraid of the Lord's verdict, even if he seems undeserving; his seeming unworthy of his office is not a charge for me to make.

Let all those listen who despise priests, let them learn the degree of respect he showed for a king. The priest, in fact, deserves far greater honor and regard than a king to the extent of the greater responsibility to which he is called. Let them learn not to judge him or call him to account, but be subject and give place to him. After all, you do not know the life of the priest, be he lowly and insignificant, whereas this man had a precise knowledge of all that Saul had done; yet even in this way he respected the responsibility given by God. Now, for proof that, even if you have a precise knowledge, you have no reason or excuse for despising those set over you or giving no heed to what they say, listen to how Christ also removed from us this pretext by what he says in the Gospels: "The scribes and the pharisees sit on the seat of Moses; so do everything they tell you to do, but as to their deeds, do not do them." [22] Do you see how he did not scorn the advice of those whose life was so corrupt as to be deserving of criticism by their disciples, nor did he reject their teaching? Now, I say this, not out of a wish to criticise the priests – perish the thought: you are witnesses of their life and utter piety; rather, my wish is that we give them great respect and honor in abundance. After all, the benefit we bring is not so much for them as for ourselves: "The one who receives a prophet in the name of a prophet, then, will receive the reward of a prophet." [23] (649) I mean, if we are commanded not to pass judgement on the lives of one another, much more on the lives of the fathers.

As I was saying, however (we must come back to this woman once more), [24] the fact that nobly bearing insults proves a source of many good things for us emerges also in what happened to Job: I do not have such admiration for him before his wife's exhortation as after that baleful advice. Let no one consider the account surprising: it frequently happens, at any rate, that people whom the normal course of events did not bring down were overcome by a corrupt word and urging. The devil also understood this, therefore, and after the trying afflictions he makes his assault through words spoken, as in fact he did also in the case of David: when he saw him nobly bearing his son's rebellion and that detestable revolt, he wished to unhinge his mind and persuade him to fall into a rage, so he set that fellow Shimei on him to get him to snap at his soul with harsh words. He got up to this mischief in Job's case as well: seeing him mocking his arrows, and like some adamantine tower resisting everything nobly, he called his wife into service so that advice might come from an unexpected quarter, and thus he concealed the harmful stratagem in her words and exaggerated the calamity. What did that noble man say, then? "Why do you speak like one of the foolish women? If we have received good things from the Lord's hand, shall we not submit to the bad?" [25] What he means is something like this: if he were not Lord, and did not so much surpass us, but were some friend of equal status, what excuse would we have, after being the beneficiary of so many favors from him, for rewarding him even with the opposite? Do you see his loving attitude towards God, and how he is not conceited or carried away with his nobly bearing those afflictions beyond the limits of human nature, nor does he think that such endurance is a mark of wisdom and magnanimity, but that he is rather paying off a necessary debt and suffering nothing out of the ordinary, and how he thus quite adequately put paid to women's talk?

This is what happened in the case of this woman as well: when he saw her nobly bearing her childlessness and casting herself on God's mercy, he set the priest's boy on her to provoke her further. The woman, however, was not affected by any of these things; instead, practised in bearing the insults at home and drilled in the taunts of her rival, she then had no trouble in being ready for such assaults. Hence she demonstrated great meekness in the temple as well, very bravely[26] and courageously putting up with the jibes about intoxication and drinking. Now, there is nothing like hearing the text itself:[27] when the boy said, "'Rid yourself of the wine, and leave the presence of the Lord,' Hannah replied in the words, 'No, sir.'" She called the one upbraiding her "sir;" she did not say what many people say, Tell me, is it the priest saying this? is the one making jokes about intoxication and drunkenness the same one who sets an example of it to others?[28] Instead, she was bent only on how to discourage the impression, especially as it was not true.

In our case frequently, on the contrary, when we are abused, and find it necessary to (650) to make excuses and clear ourselves, we start a fire, and like wild beasts we leap upon our calumniators, throttling them, dragging them into court, demanding penalties for their words, and by the very things we do confirming the impression given of us. In other words, if you wish to prove to your calumniators that you are not a drunkard, prove it by gentleness and meekness, not by insults and abuse.[28] After all, if you strike the calumniator, everyone will condemn your drunkenness, whereas if you put up with it nobly, you repel the evil suspicion through your actions – which is just what the woman also did on this occasion by saying, "No, sir," and proved in actual fact that the suspicion was false. How on earth was it that the priest came to this impression? surely he did not see her laughing? surely not dancing? surely not staggering and falling down? surely not uttering base and unseemly remarks? So where did he get that impression? It was not idly or by chance he came to it, but by the time of the day: it was midday when she was praying. How does this emerge? From the very words mentioned above: "Hannah got up after they had eaten and drunk at Shiloh, and took her place before the Lord." Do you see? The time everyone gives to rest she made a time of prayer, and after dining she betook herself to entreaty, shed floods of tears, brought to the task a mind in a state of sobriety and alertness, and after dining she prayed so fervently as to be given a gift in defiance of nature, bring childlessness to an end and correct the fault of nature.

Let us, therefore, reap this benefit from the woman so as to know how to pray after feasting: the one equipped with this knowledge will never fall into drunkenness and intoxication, will never burst from gluttony; instead, with the expectation of prayer acting as a bridle on their thoughts, they will apply due moderation to all their current concerns, and will fill both soul and body with deep blessing. The meal that begins with prayer, you see, and finishes with prayer will never fail and instead will bring us every good more liberally than a spring. Let us in no way bypass such a benefit; after all, it would be absurd if our servants, were they to take from us some part of our concerns, both thanked us and took their leave with compliments, whereas we ourselves, the beneficiaries of so many good things, did not even repay God with such respect, despite our being due to enjoy great security. Where there is prayer and thanksgiving, you see, the grace of the Holy Spirit is present, demons flee, and the whole hostile force takes to its heels and leaves the scene. The person on the point of praying does not presume to say anything out of place, even at table; and if they do say something, they quickly regret it.

Hence both at the beginning and at the end of the meal one should thank God; in particular, we should not easily fall into drunkenness, as I said before, if we developed this habit in ourselves. And so even if we get up from table with a hangover, even if drunk, let us not even then give up the habit; rather, even if thick in the head, even if tottering and falling about, [29] (651) let us keep praying even so and not desist from the habit. I mean, even if you prayed in this fashion one day, on the next day you would correct the shame of the day before. So when we are getting ready for lunch, let us remember this woman, her tears and this admirable drunkenness: the woman was drunk, not from wine, but from deep piety; after all, if she was in that condition after lunch, what would she have been like at daybreak? if she prayed so fervently after eating and drinking, what would she have been like before breaking her fast?

Let us come back to her words, then: after saying, "No, sir," she went on, "I am a woman in trouble, and have not been drinking wine or strong drink." [30] Observe how even here she makes no mention of her rival's taunts, makes no point of her evil behavior, nor exaggerates her own plight; instead, she reveals her own depression to the extent only of explaining herself to the priest. "I am a woman in trouble," she says, "I have not been drinking wine or strong drink, but am pouring out my soul before the Lord." She said, not I am praying to God, beseeching God, but "I am pouring out my soul before the Lord" – that is, I directed myself completely to God, I cleared my mind of everything but him, I made my prayer with all the force of my soul, I told God of my calamity, I laid bare my wound to him, he being in a position to apply the remedy. "Do not regard your handmaid and your daughter as a pest." [31] Once more she refers to herself as handmaid, and takes considerable trouble not to make a bad impression on the priest. She did not say to herself, What does this man's criticism mean to me? He was quite astray in his accusation, he came to the wrong impression; let my conscience be clear, and let everyone slander me. Instead, she discharged that apostolic law that bids us have in mind not only the Lord but also human beings. [32] In every way she offset the false impression by saying, "Do not regard your handmaid and your daughter as a pest." What is the meaning of "regard"? Do not consider me shameless and reckless: this outspokenness is the result of depression, not intoxication, of pain, not of drunkenness.

So what did the priest do? Note his good sense, too: he

did not inquire into the calamity, he had no wish to pry into the cause of it. Instead, what does he say? "Go in peace; may the Lord God of Israel grant you all the request you have made of him." [33] The woman turned the accuser into a supporter, such being the value of goodness and gentleness. She went off in receipt of adequate support in place of abuse, and had as patron and intercessor the one who had chided her. She did not stop at that; instead, she repeated, "May your handmaid find favor in your sight," [34] that is, May you learn from the very results and outcome of the affair that it was not from drunkenness but from such awful pain that I made my supplication and appeal. "She went off," the text says, "and no longer experienced trouble." Do you see a woman's faith? Before receiving what she asked, she had the confidence of one who had received. The reason was that she prayed with great fervor, with unhesitating ardor – hence her departure like one who had received everything. In particular, God (652) then cured her of the depression, intending to give her the gift.

Let us also imitate her, and in all our troubles have recourse to God. If we have no children, let us ask them of him; if we receive them, let us raise them with great zeal, and keep the young from all evil, especially licentiousness: it is a harsh foe, nothing being such an obstacle at that age as this passion. Let us therefore protect them on all sides with advice, exhortation, warnings and threats. If they prevail over this passion, they will not quickly succumb to a different one, but will be resistant to money, will keep control on drunkenness, will with all zeal avoid wassail and evil parties, and will be more pleasing to their parents, on the one hand, and more the object of respect to everyone, on the other. I mean, who will fail to have respect for a young person with self-control? who will fail to have an attraction and love for the one with the base passions under control? who would not choose, wealthy though they be, to give their daughter's hand with great willingness to him, though he be the most penniless of all? After all, just as no one is so desperate and abject as to wish to have as a son-in-law the man of prodigal ways and evil attachments, be he the wealthiest of all, so no one is so foolish as to reject and despise the man who is self-controlled and serious.

Let children, then, win both the respect of people and the favor of God, let us give adornment to their souls and bring them to marriage with self-control. This, in fact, is the way all the things of this life will flow to them as though from fountains, they will enjoy God's favor, and will enjoy a good name in this life and the next. May it be the good fortune of us all to enjoy it, thanks to the grace and lovingkindness of our Lord Jesus Christ, to whom with the Father and the Holy Spirit be glory, honor and power, now and forever, for ages of ages. Amen.

Homily Three

On Hannah and the rearing of Samuel,
and in proof of the value of lateness in having children
and the perils and dangers of neglecting children.

At the risk of appearing tedious and burdensome to some, I want to take up again the same theme on which I spoke to you also the other day,[1] introduce you to Hannah and direct the homily to the flowerbed of the woman's virtuous acts – a bed containing not a rose-bed or blooms that wither, but prayer and faith and great tolerance. These, in fact, are far more fragrant than spring flowers for being watered not by fountains of water but by floods of tears; fountains that come from streams do not bring gardens into bloom to the extent that floods of tears provide irrigation for the growth of prayer and cause it to climb up to the greatest height. This, then, is what happened also in the case of this woman: as soon as she opened her mouth, her prayer both rose up to heaven and brought her fruit in season, holy Samuel.

Do not be in any way upset if we begin this theme all over again: we shall not repeat the same things, (653) just some new ones so far unmentioned. I mean, in the case of a material banquet, you would provide many courses at the one sitting. Likewise we find goldsmiths making armlets, necklaces and many other golden things from the one nugget of gold: the metal may be of one kind, but the skill is manifold and is not limited by the uniformity of the material, since it is adaptable and has many uses. Now, if the events in this case are like that, more so is the grace of the Spirit; for proof that its banquet is rich in diversity listen to Paul saying, "To one is given utterance of wisdom through the Spirit, to another utterance of knowledge, to a further one faith, to another gifts of healing, support, guidance, forms of tongues. All these the one and the same Spirit activates, distributing to each one individually as he wishes."[2] Do you see the variety? There are many streams, he is saying, but one source, many courses but one host. Since the grace of the Spirit is so abundant, then, let us not tire.

Now, we saw her childless, we saw her become a mother; we saw her weeping, we saw her rejoicing; we grieved with her at one time, let us share her satisfaction today. Paul also gave that direction, "Rejoice with those who rejoice, and weep with those who weep."[3] This ought to be done not only in the case of our contemporaries but also of those living in olden times. Let no one say to me, What good do Hannah and the stories about her do me? Childless women will be able to learn how to become mothers, and mothers will in turn know what is the best way of bringing up children. And not only women: men too will gain a great deal from this story by being instructed how to be kindly disposed to their wives, even if they are affected with childlessness, as Elkanah was towards Hannah. And not only this: they will also gain something else of greater importance than this by learning that all parents should raise for God the children born to them. So just because you cannot get money or possessions from the story, let us not think it of no value to pay attention; instead, let us think it advantageous and useful for the very reason that it brings us not gold and silver but what is of greater value than they, piety of soul, it reveals to us the treasures in heaven and teaches us how to avoid every danger.

Now, while it is simple even for human beings to come up with money, by contrast setting nature to rights, dispelling depression of this kind, removing pain and lifting up a soul on the verge of collapsing is possible for no human being, but for the Lord of nature alone it is possible. In your case, if you have an incurable ailment, and have gone about the whole city spending your money and attending many physicians without finding any relief, and then you came across a woman suffering the same problem and freed from it, you would not cease imploring, beseeching, begging her to let you know the one who had freed you from it. In this case, on the contrary, when you see Hannah standing before you, describing her problem, telling you the remedy and indicating the physician without the need for imploring or beseeching, will you fail to come forward and take the remedy and listen to the whole story attentively? What good will you ever succeed in attaining? Other people by contrast (654) make long sea voyages, take on lengthy periods abroad, spend money and endure hardship for the purpose of seeing a physician in foreign parts with a reputation, and this without real confidence of being completely freed from the complaint.

You, woman,[4] on the contrary, are not on the point of taking a voyage across the seas, or of shifting to foreign parts, or of undergoing any such hardship. Why mention foreign parts? Without even having to set foot over the threshold of your house, you are able to consult your physician in your room and speak to him without an intermediary on any topic you please ("I am a God nearby," he says, remember, "and not a

God far off"),[5] and yet do you delay and hesitate? What excuse will you have? what allowance will be made for you when, though capable of finding on all sides a simple and easy release from the evils besetting you, you are slothful[6] and forfeit your own salvation? This physician, after all, can cure not only childlessness but also any kind of ailment at all both of soul and of body, should he so wish. And the remarkable feature is not only that it happens without hardship, travel, expense and intermediaries, but that he performs the cure even without pain: he does not put a stop to the problem by iron and fire, as the medical fraternity do; instead, he has only to nod, and all the depression, all the pain and the whole complaint recedes and disappears.

Let us therefore not be negligent or dilatory, even if we are needy and have fallen victim to extreme destitution. Money does not have to be laid down for us to establish our neediness: this physician requires no payment in cash – only tears, prayers and faith. If you come to him with these, you will receive all that you ask, and will go off in complete happiness. This we can learn from many sources, not least from this woman: though she did not lay out gold and silver, only prayer, faith and tears, she received what she asked and so took her leave. So let us not consider the story to be of no advantage to us: "these things were written down to instruct us on whom the ends of the ages have fallen,"[7] Scripture says, remember. Instead, let us get close to her and learn how the complaint was removed, and after its removal what she then did, and to what use she put the gift given by God.

"She sat at home and nursed Samuel,"[8] the text says. Note how she saw the child from now on not only as a child but also as consecrated; the love in her was twofold, on the one hand from nature and on the other from grace. In my view she also reverenced her own child, and rightly so: if people who intend to dedicate to God golden bowls and cups take them when ready, keep them at home before the time comes, look at them no longer as ordinary vessels but as consecrated, and no longer presume to handle them idly and casually like other vessels, (655) to a far greater extent did the woman adopt such an attitude to the child even before taking him to the temple. She loved him more, and looked after him as consecrated, considering herself sanctified through him: her house was turned into a temple, having the prophet and priest within. You can see her piety not only from her promising him, but also from her not presuming to go up to the temple before she had weaned him. "She said to her husband," the text says, remember, "'I shall not go up till the child goes up with me; when I have weaned him, he will be presented to the Lord, and will remain there forever.'" [9] Do you see? She did not think it safe to leave the house and go up: after the giving of the gift, she could not bear to be seen in public without the gift; but once she went up and took him with her, she was afraid of taking her departure. So she stayed a long time so as to bring the gift when she did appear.

She took him up, then, and left him without his being upset by being plucked from her breast. Now, you know how children are normally distressed by being weaned; but he was not distressed to be taken from his mother. Instead, he had eyes only for the Lord, who had made her a mother, and she did not grieve to be parted from the child: grace intervened and overcame the attachment from nature, each appearing to exist in harmony with the other. [10] As a vine fixed in one place extends its branches widely, and the bunches of grapes hang down at a great distance and touch the root, so too did it happen in the case of this woman: though staying at home she extended her branches as far as the temple, and suspended the ripe bunch there; distance was no problem, love agreeable to God attaching the child to the mother. Even if he was immature in age, you see, his virtue was mature, and to all who went up to the temple he proved a teacher of great godliness. After all, they made it their business to find out the manner of his birth, and took considerable heart from the hope in God. No one who saw the child went off in silence: all kept praising the one who had given him in defiance of expectation. This was the reason God deferred the birth, to augment this satisfaction, to make the woman more illustrious; those aware of her misfortune turned witnesses to God's grace, and so the great length of time she spent childless rendered her more notable and also caused her to be an object of blessing and wonder and God to be thanked on her account.

Now, I am telling you this so that, should we see holy women living in childlessness or with some other problem, we should not be upset or distressed, nor say to one another, Why on earth did God ignore a woman of such a virtuous life, and not give her a child? It is in fact not from ignoring us, but from knowing our situation more precisely than we ourselves. She went up to the temple, then, brought the lamb to the flock and the calf to the herd, and to the flowerbed the thornless rose which never withers but constantly blooms and is capable of rising to heaven itself, [11] whose fragrance everyone throughout the world (656) shares in to this day. So many years have passed, and yet her reputation for virtue of such fragrance has spread without being diminished by the passage of time, such being the nature of spiritual things.

So she went up to transplant the fine shoot; and just as hardworking farmers sow in the earth the seeds of cypresses and other such trees, then when they see the seed grown into a tree do not leave it in the same soil but pull it up from there and transfer it to another spot so that the fresh soil may welcome it into its bosom and make available its own unpolluted and comprehensive resources for the root's nourishment, so this woman also did. That is to say, the child that against all hope was sown in her womb she transferred from her home and planted in the temple, where there were constant sources of spiritual irrigation. You can see the inspired statement being fulfilled in their case which David uttered in singing thus, "Blessed the man who did not walk in the counsels of the unholy, did not take his place in the way of sinners, nor take a seat in pestilence; instead, his pleasure is in the law of the Lord, and he will meditate on his law day and night, and he will be like the tree planted on water courses, producing his fruit in due season." [12] You see, it was not a case of his coming to freedom from vice after experience of vice, but of his choosing virtue right from infancy; far from having a share in gatherings marked by lawless behavior, and a part in groups notorious for godlessness, from his very childhood he advanced from his mother's breast to a different breast of a spiritual kind. As a tree bedewed with constant moisture rises up to a great height, so this man reached the summit of virtue, by drinking constantly from attention to the divine sayings.

Let us note, however, how she planted him; let us follow the woman, let us enter into the temple with her. "She went up with him," the text says, "to Shiloh with a three year-old heifer." [13] Then the double offering occurred: one was irrational, a heifer, the other rational; while the priest sacrificed the former, the woman offered the latter – or, rather, the woman's sacrifice was better than the sacrifice the priest offered. She was, in fact, a priestess in her very being, imitating the patriarch Abraham and rivalling him for pre-eminence: whereas he took his son and descended, she let hers stay permanently in the temple – or, rather, he also made the offering in a broad sense; be sure to focus, not on the fact that he took no life, but on the fact that he saw to its completion in his will. Do you see the woman rivalling the man? do you see there was no obstacle on the part of nature to her emulating the patriarch? [14]

Let us note, however, how she offered him. "She approached the priest and said to him, 'It is I, sir.'" What is the meaning of "It is I"? Pay close attention to what is said, is the meaning: since much time had passed, she wants to remind him (657) of what was lately said – hence her words, "It is I, sir – may you live long – I am the woman who was standing in your presence in praying to the Lord for this child. I prayed to the Lord, and he granted the request I made of him. I lend him to the Lord all the days of his life to serve the Lord."[15] She did not say, I am the woman you reproached, whom you abused, whom you made fun of for drunkenness and intoxication – hence God showed you I am not drunk; it was rash of you to accuse me. None of these sharp remarks did she pass; instead, she replies with great mildness; though having her confirmation in the outcome of events, and now being in a position to reproach the priest for idly and rashly blaming her on that occasion, she did nothing of the sort, mentioning only God's beneficence. And take note of a handmaiden's prudence: when she was going through a bad time, she revealed the misfortune to no one, and did not say to the priest, I have a rival wife who though taunting and abusing me has a tribe of children, whereas despite my life of meekness I have been unable to become a mother to this very day; instead, God shut my womb, and though seeing my distress he showed no pity. She said no such thing: keeping silent on the kind of misfortune, she only indicated that she was depressed, saying, "I am a woman in trouble," and would not even have made that remark had not the priest obliged her by suspecting her of being drunk. But when God dismissed that affliction and granted her petition, then she made known the beneficence to the priest in her wish for him to be a sharer in giving thanks as he had formerly been in praying; she said, "I prayed for this child, and God granted the request I made to him. And now I lend him to the Lord."

Note the degree of moderation she employs. Do not think I am doing anything great or remarkable, she is saying, in offering the child: far from being responsible for an act of virtue, I am repaying a debt; I took a deposit, and am returning it to the giver. In saying this, she also dedicated herself along with the child, as though binding herself to the temple by a kind of cord in natural affinity. If a person's treasure, remember, is where their heart is,[16] much more was it the case that the mother's thoughts were where her child was, and her womb was filled with blessing once more. In fact, when she said these words and prayed, listen to what the priest says to Elkanah: "May the Lord repay you with another child by this woman in return for the debt in which you have placed the Lord."[17] In the beginning he did not say, May the Lord repay you, but what? "May he grant everything you ask." But after she placed the Lord in her debt, he says, "May he repay you," holding out sound hope for the future: if he gave when not in debt, much more will he repay after receiving. The first child, then, came from prayer, and those after him had their beginning in blessing; and so then the woman's entire progeny was sanctified in this way. The firstborn was of the woman's doing, whereas the second was due to her and the priest in common; as rich and fertile soil on receiving the seed (658) yields us luxuriant crops, so too the woman on receiving the priest's words in faith produced for us other flourishing offspring and cancelled the ancient curse by having children through prayer and blessing.[18]

You, then, woman, imitate her, and if you are childless, give evidence of this prayer, and appeal to the priest to join in making intercession for you; if you accept his words wholly in faith, the blessing of the fathers will result in lovely fruit in season.[19] If, on the other hand, you are a mother, consecrate your son likewise: she took him up to a temple; in your case make yourself a royal temple. Scripture says, remember, "Your members are Christ's body and the temple of the Holy Spirit within you," and again, "I shall dwell with them and walk among them."[20] I mean, how could it be other than absurd to restore an ancient dwelling about to collapse, spending money on it, assembling builders and going to all sorts of trouble, while judging the house of God (the soul of the young ought be God's house, after all) not worth even a passing thought? See that you do not hear what the Jews also once heard. When they returned from captivity, remember, saw this material temple neglected and beautified their own dwellings, they provoked God to the extent that he sent the prophet and threatened famine and extreme scarcity of necessities, and told them the reason for this threat; it was because "You live in your paneled houses, whereas my house is a ruin." [21] Now, if their mean-spirited attitude towards that temple aroused such awful wrath in God, much more will indifference to this temple provoke the Lord: it is more honorable than the other to the extent that it also contains greater signs of consecration.

So do not allow the house of God to become a den of brigands lest you hear a further threat as well, which Christ delivered to the Jews in the words, "My Father's house is a house of prayer, but you have made it a den of brigands." [22] How does it become a den of brigands? When captivating and enslaving lusts, when every kind of licentiousness we allow to enter and take a liking to the souls of the young. Such thoughts, you see, are worse than brigands, turning children's freedom into slavery, and they render them slaves to brute passions, goading them from all quarters and inflicting on their minds many wounds. For this reason let us be on the lookout daily, and by using our words as a scourge let us drive out all such passions from their soul so that the children may succeed in sharing with us the life on high and perform all the sacred rites there. Are you not aware that people living in the cities in many cases make their children, as soon as they are weaned, into games attendants, judges, and coordinators of trainers and dancers? Let us also adopt this practice; from their very earliest years let us introduce them to the way of life in heaven. After all, the earthly way of life is merely costly and brings no benefit.

(659) I mean, what benefit could there be in the mob's approval? With the fall of evening all that applause and hubbub immediately fades away, and with the passing of the festival as though carried away by a dream they are left devoid of all joy. In their search for the satisfaction that comes to them from the wreath, from the resplendent apparel and all the other paraphernalia, they would not succeed in finding it, as it has all departed more swiftly than any breeze.

The way of life in heaven is quite the opposite: it brings us great and lasting benefit without any expense. It is not inebriates, you see, but the choir of angels that applauds the one living there. Why mention the choir of angels? The Lord of the angels himself will commend and welcome them. The person commended by God is crowned and celebrated, not for one or two or three days, but for all eternity, and you would never see the head of such a person bereft of that glory; far from being confined to set days, the period of that festival lasts for the immortality of the future. Neediness could never be an obstacle to sacred ritual; on the contrary, it is possible even for the needy to celebrate this sacred ritual, and especially the needy in that they are freed of all this world's vanity, the requirement being not outlay of money and affluence but a pure and continent mind. From this it is that the dress for that way of life is woven for the soul and the wreath plaited, and so unless it were adorned with the works of virtue, no benefit would come to it from gold in abundance, just as no harm would ensue from poverty if it has its wealth stored within. Let not only the boys but also the girls celebrate this sacred ritual; it is not a case, after all, as in public life, of men alone being called upon to perform these services: this display involves also women, the elderly and the young, slaves and free. After all, where the soul is on show, neither sex nor age nor earthly station nor anything else constitutes an obstacle.[23]

Hence I exhort you all to expose both sons and daughters from their earliest years to these sacred rituals and store up for them riches suited to such a way of life, not digging up gold or amassing silver, but depositing in their soul goodness, self-control, seriousness and every other virtue, the sacred ritual requiring this outlay. If, then, we amass this resource both for ourselves and for the children, we shall enjoy great notoriety in the present life, and in the future life we shall hear that blessed call by which Christ celebrates all who confess him. Now, confession is not only through faith but also through works, with the result that should the latter be missing, we run the risk of being punished along with those who deny him. There is not one way of denying, after all, but many and varied, as Paul described them to us in writing in these terms, "They confess they know God, but deny him in practice," and again, "Anyone who does not provide for relatives, especially of their own household, has denied the faith, and is worse than an unbeliever," and again, "Shun avarice, (660) which is idolatry." [24] Since the forms of denial are as numerous, therefore, so too are the forms of confession, and much more so. Let us all be zealous in adopting these forms of confessing so that we ourselves may enjoy honor in heaven, thanks to the grace and lovingkindness of our Lord Jesus Christ, to whom with the Father and the Holy Spirit be glory, now and forever, for ages of ages. Amen.

Homily Four

*Against those who absent themselves from the assemblies and go
to the spectacles,
and in proof that time spent in church is not only more useful
but also more pleasant than attendance at spectacles,
and on the second part of Hannah's prayer,* [1]
*and on the need to pray at all times and in every place,
whether we be in the market place, on the road, or in bed.*

I am at a loss to know what words to employ today: seeing the assemblies less well attended, Old Testament readings scorned, New Testament readings bypassed, fathers despised, the insult passing from the servants to the Lord, my intention on the one hand is to castigate, while on the other I recognise that those who should hear the accusation are not present – only you, who do not need this exhortation and correction. [2] Yet we should not be silent, either: we shall cause the slight resentment against them to go into thin air by expelling it in words, and shall also make them ashamed of themselves and blush by letting loose on them as many accusers as all you listeners here. I mean, if they had been present here, they would have heard only us reproving them, whereas in fact by avoiding our reproof they will hear it all from you. This is what friends do, too: when they do not find the guilty ones, they meet up with their friends so that they may go off and report their words. God did this, too: leaving aside those who had sinned against him, he accosted Jeremiah, who had done nothing wrong, and said, "Did you see what the foolish daughter, Judah, did to me?" [3]

This is the very reason that we, too, are taking up the matter in their regard with you, so that you may go off and correct them. After all, who would put up with such a slight? [4] We gather here only once a week, and they cannot manage to set aside their worldly concerns even on that day. If you offer a reproof, they at once pretend neediness, daily necessities, pressing occupations, thus proposing an excuse worse than any accusation: what could be more damning than this accusation, that something seems more urgent and pressing to you than God's affairs? Particularly, then, is it the case that, even if this were true, the excuse would be an accusation, as I said; but for you to learn that it is a pretext and pretence and cover for indifference, [5] the day after tomorrow will convict them all of putting up such an excuse, without my saying a word, when the whole city decamps to the racecourse, [6] and homes and markets are left empty for the sake of this lawless spectacle. Here in church you can see that not even the front seats are taken, whereas there not only the racecourse but also upstairs, private homes, roofs, crannies and countless other places are taken over. (661) Not even neediness, work, bodily infirmity, sore feet or anything else of the kind inhibits this irrepressible frenzy; the elderly betake themselves off there with greater eagerness than the young and healthy, bringing their grey hairs into disrepute, making a mockery of their age and turning their seniority into a laughing stock. Whereas when they attend here they think they are suffering even to the point of choking, and faint when they listen to the divine sayings, claiming cramped conditions and stifling heat and the like, there on the contrary they even endure the sun with head bared, trodden on, pushed, tightly packed together and subjected to countless other inconveniences, and yet feel as though lolling about in a meadow. [7]

This is the reason our cities are corrupt: they are vicious teachers of the young. I mean, how could you develop self-control in the young person aprey to disorder and licentiousness when you yourself at your age carry on in this way, when you yourself after such a length of time have not had your fill of such a hideous spectacle? how could you discipline your son, how punish your sinful servant, how advise someone else who neglects their duty when you are guilty of such shameful behavior in extreme old age? If a young person insults the elderly, immediately the plea of age is raised, and countless fellow plaintiffs rally around, whereas when the old ought bring self-control to the young and prove a kind of norm of virtue, there is no mention of age then: they betake themselves to the lawless spectacle with greater zest than the young themselves. Now, I say this and point the finger at older people, not to discharge the young of criticism and complaint, but by those means to render them safe: if it is inappropriate for the old, much more so for the young. I mean, to the former group apply much ridicule and deeper shame, whereas in the latter case the damage is worse, the ruin abysmal to the extent that the urges of lust are more potent in the young and the flame more scorching in them, and even if it has less material to work with, it sets it all ablaze. In other words, the young are more easily inclined to passion and lust – hence the need for greater watchfulness, a tighter rein, a more secure barricade and curb.

Do not tell me this, mortal that you are, that the spectacle brings pleasure: show me how it does not bring harm along with the pleasure. Why mention harm? Proof that the event does not even bring pleasure you will clearly learn from this. On your return from those awful races, meet up with those returning from church, and carefully study who is enjoying greater satisfaction: the one who heard the inspired authors, shared in the blessing, enjoyed the instruction, made petition to God for their sins, rendered their conscience clearer and weighed themselves down with no such guilt [8] – or you, who abandoned your mother, scorned the inspired authors, insulted God, danced with the devil, listened to people uttering blasphemies and profanities, wasted time to no purpose, and have nothing to bring home from there of bodily or spiritual benefit? And so even for pleasure's sake you should choose to meet here: at the other place there is immediate condemnation, accusation by (662) conscience, repentance for what happened, shame, reproach, and the inability to raise one's eyes, whereas here it is quite the opposite – frankness, free speech, and conversing openly with everyone about all that was heard here.

So when you rush into the marketplace and see everyone heading off to that awful spectacle, betake yourself at once to church, spend a little time there and enjoy the divine words without interruption. You see, if you are swept up by the crowd and head off to the other place, you will gain little satisfaction and regret it all that day, the following day and for many others, condemning yourself, whereas if you keep a grip on yourself for a while, you will be able to enjoy yourself all day. This normally happens, of course, not only in this case but also in all others: while vice offers some passing pleasure but endless pain, virtue by contrast offers brief hardship but endless benefit together with happiness. For example, one person prayed to God, wept, grieved for a short time in prayer; another person enjoyed themselves all through the day, then gave alms, fasted, practised some other form of good works, or was insulted without retaliating; being patient for at least a brief moment and checking anger, they are permanently happy and joyful by recalling their own virtuous actions. It is quite the contrary with vice: someone insults or retaliates; later at home they eat their heart out recalling the words which in many cases brought great harm. And so, if it is pleasure you are after, "Shun youthful desires,"[9] practise self-control and make attention to the divine sayings your pursuit.

I say this to you so that you may speak to those people, overwhelm with these words, draw them away from every wicked habit and persuade them to do everything with the proper attitude. After all, you would not find commendable the zeal in people whose behaviour is idle and reckless; I shall establish this from tomorrow's assembly. I mean, when holy Pentecost is celebrated by us, so big a crowd will hasten to attend that our whole place will be packed; but I do not place much importance on size: it comes from habit, not piety. What could be more wretched than those people, in fact, when their indifference involves them in such recriminations and their apparent zeal is devoid of commendation? In other words, the one who takes part in this divine assembly with fervor and desire should do so consistently, and not be amongst those showing up only on feastdays and in turn go off with them, simply driven like sheep.

I succeeded, then, in extending the homily's opening to even greater length; but since I am aware that you will say the proper things to them in place of our admonition, and will tell them more than was said in case I should seem to go overboard in upbraiding them, I shall leave the rest to you, and come to the customary instruction, (663) continuing the account of the story of Hannah. Don't be surprised if we are not yet rid of this theme: I can't get this woman out of my mind, so amazed am I at her beauty of soul and charm of thought. I mean, I am attracted by her eyes weeping in prayer, always attentive, her lips and mouth not reddened with some coating but enhanced with thanksgiving to God as hers were; I admire her for her sound values, and I am more amazed that as a woman she had sound values – woman, whom many frequently criticise. "From a woman was the beginning of sin," Scripture says, remember, "and because of her we all die," and again, "Any vice is insignificant compared with a woman's vice," [10] and Paul, "Adam was not deceived, remember: the woman was deceived, and fell into transgression." [11] The reason I particularly admire her is that she escaped the charges, she put aside the accusation, that though a member of the maligned and criticised sex she repelled all the reproaches, teaching in deed the lesson that even women did not become like that by nature but by choice and their own mean-spiritedness, and that it is possible for this sex to attain the heights of virtue. This creature, after all, is contentious and highly strung, and if she inclines to wickedness, she commits great evil; if she attains virtue, she will give up her life before forsaking her purpose. [12]

In this case, at any rate, she both overcame her nature and got the better of innate urging, and with the insistence of her prayer she caused a child to spring from her deadened womb. Hence once more she has recourse to petition, and after its being granted she speaks thus, "My heart was strengthened in the Lord, my horn was exalted in my God." [13] On the meaning, then, of "My heart was strengthened in my Lord" I spoke to you the other day, dearly beloved, you remember;

now I must comment on the remaining text. After saying, "My heart was strengthened in the Lord," note, she added, "My horn was exalted in my God." What is the meaning of "my horn"? Scripture frequently employs this phrase, remember, as when it says, "His horn was exalted" and "The horn of his anointed was exalted." [14] So what on earth does "horn" mean? Force, glory, prominence, using a metaphor from the brute beasts: God implanted in them only the horn by way of glory and weaponry, and if they lose it, they lose most of their force; and like a soldier without weapons a bull without horns is also easily disposed of. So by this the woman means nothing other than this, My glory is exalted. How is it exalted? "In my God," she says. Hence the exaltation is also secure, having a firm and permanent root: while glory from human beings corresponds to the baseness of those glorifying, and so is very liable to disappear, God's glory is not like that, remaining forever permanent.

To suggest both of these ideas – the fragility of the former and the permanence of the latter – the inspired author spoke this way, "All flesh is grass, and all human glory is like the flower of the grass. The grass has dried up, and the flower fallen." What are the terms in which he speaks about God's glory, if not these? "The word of the Lord, by contrast, abides forever." [15] And it is clear that was true also of this woman: kings and generals and rulers, (664) who often go to much trouble to ensure their memory is imperishable, building lavish tombs, [16] erecting statues and numerous images everywhere, and leaving countless memorials of their deeds, are never heard of again and there is no one who knows even of their mere name, whereas the praises of this woman are sung everywhere in the world today. Should you go to Scythia, Egypt, the Indies, even to the very ends of the world, you would hear everyone praising this woman's deeds, and in short wherever the sun shines on the earth, the glory of Hannah has made its mark. This alone is not surprising, that the woman's praises are sung everywhere in the world, but also that despite the passage of so long a time not only has commendation of her not died out but has even increased and grown to much greater dimensions. Everyone is familiar with her sound values, her endurance and patience, in cities and in the country, in homes and in encampments, on ships and in work places – everywhere you will hear this woman eulogised. You see, whenever God wishes to glorify someone, even if death intervenes, or length of time or anything else at all, the bloom of that glory abides forever, with no one succeeding in obscuring this notoriety. [17]

Hence this woman also, who teaches all the listeners the lesson of the need for recourse not to what is passing but to the source of goods that abide fixed and immovable for us, mentioned the basis of glory: after saying, "My heart is strengthened in the Lord," she went on, "My horn is exalted in my God," suggesting to us by this the twofold goods, which rarely come together. In other words, I was freed from my turmoil, she is saying, I put aside my dishonor, I enjoyed security, I had a share in glory. You would not easily see both these things being combined: many people are freed from dangers, but do not have notable life; others in turn enjoy glory and notoriety, but are obliged to be at risk on account of this glory. For example, in many cases people confined to prison – adulterers, sorcerers, grave robbers and criminals guilty of other crimes – are then released from their confinement by some royal pardon; while they are rid of punishment, they are not acquitted of reproach, and instead have the shame clinging to them. In other cases noble soldiers take on the life of glory and fame, making themselves available in risky fashion for warfare, and they often sustain numerous wounds and undergo an untimely death; in their desire for glory they sacrifice their safety.

In the woman's case, on the contrary, both these things came together: she enjoyed security and attained glory. This happened also in the case of the three young men: they were freed from danger by escaping the fire, and they became famous for overcoming the force of the element in defiance of nature.[18] God's actions are like that: he makes a gift of a life that is at once both illustrious and secure. Both these aspects, then, she hinted at in saying, "My heart is strengthened in the Lord, my horn is exalted in my God." She did not say simply "in God" but "in my God," appropriating the common Lord of the world to herself. This she did, not to diminish his (665) lordship, but to demonstrate and confirm her personal love. That is the way with lovers, after all: they are not content to love like the general run of people; instead, they insist on showing their affection exclusively and individually. David also acted in this fashion in saying, "O God my God, I rise early to pray to you:"[19] after mentioning his common lordship, he mentions also his individual care for the saints. And again, "O God my God, hearken to me: why have you abandoned me?"[20] And again, "I shall say to God, You are my protector."[21] These words are the mark of an ardent and fervent soul motivated by longing.

That is the way this woman also behaved. While, however, the fact that human beings do this is not surprising, be amazed when you see God doing it. I mean, just as the former do not call upon him in common with the general run of people, but individually want him to be their own God, so too he on his part does not say he is their God only in common with the general run of people but also theirs individually. Hence he says, "I am the God of Abraham and Isaac and Jacob,"[22] not to reduce his lordship but rather to extend it: it is not the number of those under his rule but the virtue of those accepting his kingship that demonstrates his rule, nor does he rejoice so much in being called God of heaven and earth, of sea and what is in it as he rejoices in being called God of Abraham and Isaac and Jacob. What happens in the case of human beings you can see occurring in the case of God as well; for example, with human beings slaves are called after their masters, and it is customary for everyone to speak in these terms, So-and-so the custodian belonging to so-and-so, So-and-so the manager belonging to the general or lieutenant so-and-so. No one says, So-and-so the lieutenant belonging to this custodian: we always call the less important after the more important. But in God's case the opposite happens: not only is Abraham said to belong to God, but also God to Abraham, the Lord called after his servant.

This at any rate was the very thing Paul, too, was struck by in saying, "For this reason God is not ashamed to be called their God;" the Lord is not ashamed, he is saying, to be named after his servants. Why is he not ashamed? He gave the reason, namely, for us to imitate him. "But they were strangers and sojourners," he says. [23] This actually is a reason to be ashamed: the stranger seems to be lowly and despicable. Those holy ones were not strangers in the way we think, however, but in a different and baffling way: we give the name strangers to those who have left their own country and gone to another land, whereas they were not strangers in that fashion; instead, they despised the whole world, considered this land to be puny, and set their sights on the city in the heavens, not out of conceit but out of magnanimity, not from folly but from love of wisdom. You see, since they took a hard look at everything on earth, and recognised that it was all passing away and perishing, with nothing here-below permanent and immovable – not wealth, not influence, not glory, not life itself – and instead each of them having an end and moving quickly to its termination, whereas things in heaven are not like this but are unending and immortal, they preferred to be strangers to what is passing away and receding so as to take hold of that which abides. They were strangers, therefore, not for not having a country but for hankering after a country that abides forever. This is what the author (666) indicated, then, in saying, "Those saying this make clear they are looking for a homeland." Tell me, which homeland? is it the former one, which they left? No, he says: "After all, if they had in mind that one, they would have had the opportunity to return; but as it is, they long for a better one, namely, a heavenly one, whose architect and builder is God. Hence God is not ashamed to be called their God." [24]

Let us also imitate them, I beseech you; let us despise present realities, [25] let us long for the future, let us take this woman as a mentor, always have recourse to God and ask everything of him. Nothing, you see, equals prayer: it makes the impossible possible, the difficult easy, and renders the crooked way straight. Blessed David also practised it, and hence said, "Seven times a day I praised you for the judgements of your righteousness." [26] Now, if a king, a man immersed in countless concerns and beset from every quarter, beseeches God so many times a day, what excuse or pardon would we have, with so much free time on our hands, not to implore him incessantly, especially as this puts us in a position to reap such benefit? It is inconceivable, in fact, inconceivable that someone praying with due fervor and constantly beseeching God should ever sin. Why this is so, I shall tell you. The person who enkindles his attention, lifts up his soul, transports himself to heaven, and thus calls upon his Lord, remembering his sin, speaking to him about pardon for them and begging him to be merciful and mild sets aside every worldly concern through the time spent in this converse, takes wing and becomes exalted above the human passions. He is not distracted by the sight, even of a comely woman, [27] the ardor of his prayer abiding within him and dispelling every untoward thought. Being human, however, it is likely that you relapse even into sloth when an hour or two or three has passed after prayer, and you notice the ardor you have developed about to evaporate gradually; then betake yourself promptly to prayer again and rekindle your cooling attention.

If you do this throughout the day, maintaining your fervor at intervals with the frequency of your prayers, you will not give the devil an occasion and admission to assault your thoughts. And as we do when having lunch and on the point of taking a drink, when we notice the hot water has cooled down, we put it on the stove again for it to be quickly heated, let us act likewise in this case also, and by giving our mouth to prayer as though onto hot coals, let us rekindle our mind once again with piety. Let us imitate the builders: when they are getting ready to build with bricks, on account of the fragility of the material they support the building with long timbers, doing this not at great intervals but at short ones so as to make the binding of the bricks firmer through the closeness of these timbers. Do this in your case, too, and (667) fence your life around on every side by interspersing your worldly activities with constant prayers as though with wooden binding. If, then, you act in this way, even should countless winds later blow, even should trials, discouragement, disagreeable thoughts of some kind, trouble of whatever sort befall, they will not succeed in demolishing that house held together in this way by frequent prayers.

How is it possible, you ask, for a man of the world, tied to the bench, to pray three times a day and betake himself to church? It is possible and quite simple: even if heading off to church is not manageable, it is possible even for the man tied to the bench to stand there in the vestibule and pray. After all, there is not such need for words as for thoughts, for outstretched hands as for a disciplined soul, for deportment as for attitude, since Hannah herself was heard not for uttering a loud and clear cry but for calling out loudly inside in the heart: "Her voice was not audible, but the Lord hearkened to her," [28] the text says, note. Many other people also did this in many cases, despite the officer calling out from inside, threatening, ranting and raving, while they stood in the porch making the sign of the cross and saying a few prayers in their mind, and then going in and transforming and soothing him, turning him from wild to mild. They were not prevented from praying like this by the place or the time or the absence of words. Do likewise yourself: groan deeply, recall your sins, gaze towards heaven, say in your mind, "Have mercy on me, O God," [29] and you have completed your prayer. The one who said "Have mercy," after all, gave evidence of confession, and acknowledged their own sins: it belongs to sinners to have mercy shown. The one who said "Have mercy on me" received pardon for their faults: the one to whom mercy has been shown is not punished. The one who said "Have mercy" attained the kingdom of heaven: the one on whom God will have mercy he not only frees from sin but also judges worthy of the future goods.

Accordingly, let us not make excuses, claiming a house of prayer [30] is not close by: if we have the right dispositions, the grace of the Spirit made us personally temples of God, and there is ease for us in every respect. Our worship, after all, is not of the kind that formerly prevailed among the Jews, which was long on appearance but short on reality. In that case, you see, the worshiper had to go up to the temple, buy a turtle-dove, get hold of wood and fire, take sword in hand, appear before the altar, and carry out many other requirements. In our case, on the other hand, it is not like that: wherever you are, you have the altar with you, the sword, and the victim, you yourself being priest and altar and victim. In other words, wherever you are, you can set up the altar, giving evidence only of an attentive will, place being no an obstacle, time no hindrance; even if you do not go down on your knees, do not strike your breast or raise your hands to heaven, (668) and merely demonstrate an ardent disposition, you have completed the whole of the prayer. It is possible for a woman with distaff in hand working at the loom to gaze towards heaven in her mind and call upon God with ardor; it is possible for a man venturing into the marketplace and walking by himself to pray with attention, and for someone else seated at the workbench sewing skins to direct his soul to the Lord; it is possible for a servant making purchases and running hither and yon, or standing in the kitchen, when there is no possibility of going to church, to pray attentively and ardently. Place is not something God is ashamed of: he looks for one thing only, a fervent mind and sober spirit.

For you to learn that there is no need at all of appearance or places or times, but of a generous and ardent disposition, Paul was lying on his back in prison and not standing up (the stocks fastening his feet did not allow it, after all) when the prison shook while he was praying zealously as he lay down, the foundations were moved, the guard was terrified, and Paul later conducted him to the sacred rites of initiation. [31] Likewise Hezekiah was not standing upright nor on his knees, but was lying on his back in bed on account of sickness, facing the wall, when he ardently called on God with a sober spirit, recalled the sentence passed on him, won a great favor and regained his former good health. [32] You would find this happening not only with holy and important men [33] but also with wicked ones: the brigand was not standing in a house of prayer nor on his knees, but stretched out on the cross, when with a few words he attained to the kingdom of heaven; [34] another man was in a deep pit, [35] another in a den of wild beasts, [36] still another in the very belly of a sea monster, [37] when calling upon God they dispelled all the troubles besetting them and won favor from on high.

In saying this, I exhort you unceasingly to keep up the habit of visiting the churches and praying at home in tranquillity, and when time allows going on your knees and stretching out your hands. If, however, we are caught up by reason of time or place with a crowd of people, let us not on that account abandon prayer, but in the fashion I mentioned to your good selves pray and beseech God in the conviction of gaining your petition nonetheless with that prayer. I said as much, not for you to applaud and marvel, but for you to practise this yourselves, night time and day time, interspersing the time of work with prayers and petitions. [38] If we manage our affairs this way, we shall both pass this life securely and also attain the kingdom of heaven. May it be the good fortune of us all to attain it, thanks to the grace and lovingkindness of our Lord Jesus Christ, to whom with the Father and the Holy Spirit be the glory, now and forever, for ages of ages. Amen.

Homily Five

*Against those who come together only on feast-days,
and what a feast-day is;
and against those carping at God's providence, on account of
there being rich and poor people in this life;
and in proof of the fact that poverty is most useful
and that it brings greater pleasure and security
in all situations than wealth;
and on Hannah.*

It was all to no avail, apparently, for us to appeal to those who joined us in the previous assembly, urging them to remain in their paternal home, and not attend and then absent themselves along with those who appear before us only on a feast-day. Or rather it was not to no avail: even if none of them was convinced by what was said, yet our fee is paid up and the requirements of a defence before God have been met. This is the reason that the speaker, whether people pay heed or not, must cast the seed and deposit the money so that the debt with God may no longer be in his name but in the bankers'. That is what we in fact did by accusing, reproving, exhorting, admonishing. We brought to mind, remember, the son who had squandered his substance and returned to his father's home, and we highlighted all the hardship, the hunger, the shame, the reproaches and all the other things he endured in foreign parts in our wish to bring them to a

better frame of mind with this example. Far from stopping
short at that point, we brought out also the father's affection
for them, not insisting on their liability for indifference but
receiving them with open arms, offering pardon for their
failings, opening the door, laying the table, clothing them in
the robe of teaching, and providing them with every other
form of attention. On their part, however, they did not imitate
that famous son or condemn themselves for their former
departure, nor did they stay in the paternal home; instead,
they absented themselves again.[1]

It would therefore have been up to you – you who are
always with us[2] – to bring them back and convince them to
share the feast-day with us at each assembly. Even if Pentecost
has gone by, you see, still the feast-day has not gone by: every
gathering is a feast-day. What is the evidence for this? The
very words of Christ, in which he says, "Where two or three
are gathered in my name, there am I in the midst of them."[3]
Now, when Christ is in the midst of those assembled together,
what further proof of this feast do you look for that is more
convincing? Where there is instruction and prayers, blessings
of the fathers and attention to divine laws, meeting of
brethren and binding together in true love, converse with
God and God's speaking to human beings, how could it be
other than a feast-day and festal assembly? It is not size of
the assembly, after all, that normally makes feast-days but
the virtue of those assembled, not the riches of the garments
but the charm of piety, not the extravagance of the banquet
but the care of the soul; the most important thing to celebrate,
you see, is a good conscience. It is like secular parties: people
with no splendid clothes to wear or particularly extravagant
banquet to enjoy, living instead in poverty and starvation
and extreme difficulty, are not (670) aware of the time of
celebration, even should they see the whole city dancing;
instead, they are all the more distressed and reduced to tears
as they see everybody else enjoying themselves while they

personally are suffering want. The rich, on the other hand, with their luxurious life and many changes of clothes, and enjoying great satisfaction, even should the festal period not have arrived, think it time to celebrate. It is similar also in spiritual affairs: the person living in righteousness and the practice of virtue, even should it not be a feast-day, celebrates a feast by reaping the benefit of untainted satisfaction from conscience, whereas the person given to sin and vice and conscious of the evil within is least of all in the mood for celebrating, even should it be a feast-day.

And so it is possible for us, if we wish it, to celebrate a feast every day provided we practise virtue and keep a clear conscience. After all, what does the past assembly have over and beyond the present one? is there anything beyond hubbub and disorder? I mean, when there is also reception of the holy sacraments and sharing in the other spiritual rites – I refer to things like prayer, listening, blessings, kiss of peace and all the rest, the same as today – this day will be in no respect inferior to that one, neither for you nor for me as speaker.⁴ After all, the people who listened to us then are the ones who are about to listen to us now, though those not present now were likewise not present then, even if they seemed to be present in body. They are not listening now – or, rather, they did not listen even then – and not only did they not listen: they even made things difficult for the listeners by creating hubbub and disorder. And so in my view the spectacle then and now is of the same kind, the congregation the same, this one in no way inferior to that. If, however, we must remark on something that is also noteworthy, this one has something better than the other in that the address is uninterrupted, the instruction undisturbed, the listening accompanied by greater understanding, with no hubbub to make your attention difficult.

Now, I say this with no disrespect for the congregation

assembled here: I want to persuade you not to be discouraged or downcast at the small numbers of those assembled here now. We are not interested, you understand, in seeing a large number of bodies in church but a large number of listeners. So since we have the same guests then and now, we shall set the meal before you with the same enthusiasm today as well, returning to the theme that the festal period interrupted. I mean, as it would have been inappropriate at the occurrence of Pentecost [5] for us to fail to speak on the good things coming our way at that time and keep to the former theme, so now with the passing of Pentecost we shall properly resume the thread of the story, picking up the theme to do with Hannah. The question, you see, is not the number of things said and the number of days it has taken, but whether we are approaching the end of our treatment. Those who find a treasure, remember, even should they take many objects from it, do not desist until they have exhausted it, as it is natural for them to make it their own, not by taking many objects but by leaving nothing behind. Now, if those mad about money adopt such zeal in connection with things that perish and do not last, (671) much more should we behave like that in regard to the divine treasures, not desisting until we have exhausted all that becomes obvious to us. I said what becomes obvious since it is beyond us to exhaust everything: the efficacy of the divine thoughts is an ever-flowing stream, never failing or running dry.

Let us not tire, then: our homily is not about ordinary matters, but about prayer, our hope – prayer, through which the barren woman became a mother, the childless one had many children, the sorrowful one found joy; through it natural incapacity was set to rights, a closed womb opened, and all impossible things became possible. Hence let us comment on everything in detail, explicating every sentence so as not to pass over even the slightest detail, as far as possible. [6] For this very reason we spent two whole addresses on two solitary sentences, the first, "My heart is strengthened in the Lord," and then the second, "My horn is exalted in my God." It follows that today we go on to the third. What is that? "My mouth was opened wide against my foes," it says, "I rejoiced in your salvation." [7] Attend to the precision of the expression: she did not say, My mouth was sharpened against my foes; it was not readied for insults and jibes, not for taunts and accusation, but for exhortation and advice, for correction and admonition. Hence she did not say, My tongue was sharpened against my foes, but "was opened wide." I have enjoyed relief, she is saying, I am able to exercise free speech; now I have escaped shame, my confidence has returned. At this point she did not even mention the rival wife by name, simply using a general term, as though suppressing the identity of the person who had caused her so much grief. She did not say, as many women do say, God has shamed her, he has confounded and brought down this brutal, haughty and big-talking woman – simply, "My mouth was opened wide against my enemies, I rejoiced in your salvation."

See how she observes the same law right throughout the prayer: as she said in the beginning, "My heart is strengthened in the Lord, my horn is exalted in my God, my mouth is opened wide against my foes," so at this point, too, "I rejoiced in your salvation." Not simply "in salvation," but "in your salvation;" I rejoice and am glad, she is saying, not for being saved, but for being saved through you. This is what the saints' prayers are like: more than in his gifts they rejoice in the God giving them; it is not so much that they love him for his works as they love them for his sake. This is a mark of grateful servants, this of thankful slaves, preferring their Lord to all their own possessions. Let us also, I beseech you, have this disposition: if we commit sin, let us not be distressed for being punished but for provoking the Lord; if we practise virtue, let us not rejoice on account of the kingdom of heaven but for being pleasing to the king of heaven. To a person of this mentality, in fact, offending God is more to be feared than any hell, just as pleasing God is more to be desired than any kingdom. Do not be surprised if this is the way to be disposed to God when even in the case of human beings many people have this disposition. Often, at any rate, we have children who are true; should we unwittingly annoy them, we punish (672) and chastise ourselves; and we do this also in the case of friends.

Now, if in the case of friends and children we think distressing them is far worse than being punished, much more should this be our attitude in the case of God, and we should think that doing anything not pleasing to him is worse than any hell. Blessed Paul was like this: he said, "I am convinced that not angels, principalities, or powers, not the present or the future, not height or depth or any other created thing will succeed in separating us from the love of God, which is in Christ Jesus our Lord."[8] In our case, too, when we declare the holy martyrs blessed, we bless them first for their wounds, and then for their reward; for their stripes, and then for the crowns laid up for them: the rewards have their origin and basis in the wounds, not the wounds in the rewards. Blessed Paul likewise rejoiced in the troubles befalling him for Christ's sake ahead of the good things laid up for him, and said as much in loud tones, "I rejoice in the sufferings for you," and again, "Not only that, but we boast also in the tribulations," and again, "Because it was granted to us by God, not only to believe in him, but also to suffer for him."[9] It really is the greatest grace, in fact, the perfect crown and reward not inferior to the recompense to come, being thought worthy of suffering something for Christ; all those know this who truly and ardently know how to love Christ.

This woman was also someone like this, having an ardent longing for God and a burning love – hence her saying, "I rejoiced in your salvation:" far from having anything in common with the earth, she despised all human help, was given wings and lifted on high by the grace of the Spirit, she had her eyes fixed on God in everything, and looked there for her solution to her present problems. She knew, you see, she knew clearly that human gifts of whatever kind resemble the nature of those who give them; there is need everywhere of grace from on high if, that is, we intend to lower anchor securely. For this reason she also had recourse to him in everything, and though receiving a gift she rejoiced rather in the giver, and said with thanksgiving, "There is no one holy like the Lord, and no one righteous like our God, and there is no one holy besides you." [10] His judgement is incomprehensible, you see, his decision pure and infallible.

Do you see the attitude of a prudent soul? I mean, she did not say to herself, What a marvelous thing has happened to me! How much more important than other people! What my rival received in the past in abundance I enjoy after a long delay, with effort and tears, with supplication, entreaty and great hardship. Instead, after showing a commendable trust in God's providence, she does not call the Lord to account for what happened, as do the general run of people, daily passing judgement on God: whether it is the rich they see or the needy, they direct countless attacks against his providence. What are you up to, mortal that you are? Paul did not allow you to pass judgement even on your fellow servant, (673) speaking in these terms, "So do not make any judgement before the time, until the Lord comes" [11] – and do you haul the Lord before the tribunal and demand an account of his doings, without fear or trembling? What pardon would you win, what excuse, tell me, when despite being in receipt of such wonderful examples of his providence by the day and by the hour you pass sentence on the basis of apparent inequalities between riches and poverty against the good order in all things, and wrongly as well? I mean, should you choose to examine even these things with the proper attitude and careful attention, even if there were nothing else to recommend God's providence, riches and poverty most of all would clearly demonstrate it. After all, were you to do away with poverty, you would do away with the whole fabric of life and would destroy our way of living: there would be no sailors, no steersmen, no farmers, no builders, no weavers, no shoemakers, no architects, no metalworkers, no leatherworkers, no bakers, no craftsmen of any type; and with none of these available, all our life would disappear. As it is, you see, the pressure of poverty, like an excellent teacher, falls upon each of these and urges them to work, albeit unwillingly, whereas if all were destined to be rich, all would be destined to live in idleness, and thus everything would perish and be lost. [12]

It is likewise easy to reduce them to silence independently of this by another tack, namely, from their own words of accusation. I mean, why is it, tell me, that you criticise God's providence? because one person has more money and one less? So what? If we were to demonstrate the equal lot befalling all people in basic matters and far greater ones that constitute our lives, would you concede God's providence? Necessarily so. After all, if you cite as an example of the lack of providence the fact that people do not enjoy equally one thing, namely, money, should all be shown to enjoy equally not one thing, paltry as it is, but many things of far greater value, it is obvious that you would be obliged to concede from that the providence of God, willy-nilly. So, come now, let us move in our argument to the things that constitute our life, examine them precisely, and see whether in that respect the wealthy are better off than the poor. For example, the wealthy have Thasian wine and many other beverages brewed and served with spices; the springs of water, on the other hand, are available to everyone, rich and poor alike. Perhaps you are amused to hear this equality; learn, then, how far more important by nature is water than wine, more basic and more useful, and then you will have second thoughts and realise the true wealth of the poor. You see, if wine were not available, no great harm would come to anyone, with the single exception of the infirm, whereas were you to stop the springs and do away with that basic necessity, you would overcome our life altogether and destroy all the arts; we would not last even two days, but would meet a speedy end of a most miserable and awful kind.

And so in basic necessities that constitute our life the poor are no worse off; rather, paradoxically, they are better off than the wealthy. In fact, you can find many rich people suffering bodily disorders due to their luxurious lifestyle and general abstinence from water, whereas the poor (674) all through life enjoy without worry this liquid like streams of honey, and so they betake themselves to the sources of water and expect to get from there an enjoyment that is untainted and pure. And what about fire's natural qualities? is it not more basic than countless treasures and any human resource? This useful treasure is likewise available equally to rich and poor. And the benefit coming to our bodies from the air, and the sun's rays – surely it is not accessible in a greater degree to the wealthy and less to the poor, the former seeing it with four eyes, the latter only with two? You could not claim this, either: the measure of enjoyment has been determined equally for both rich and poor – or, rather, in this case as well you could find the poor better off than the rich to the extent that they have sharper senses, keener eyes and more precise observation overall. Hence they also gain the benefit of truer enjoyment, and to a greater degree revel in and enjoy the perception of nature.

It is not only in the case of the elements but also of the other good things given us by nature where you will recognise great equality – or, rather, the advantage accruing to the poor. Sleep, for example, sweeter and more basic than any kind of luxury, and more useful than any kind of food, is easier for the poor than the rich: for the latter constant luxury normally puts a stop to enjoyment in everything – in eating from being hungry, in drinking from being thirsty, in sleeping from being tired – as it is not so much the nature of the exercise as the pressure of necessity that constitutes the pleasure in each of these cases. At any rate, drinking sweet and fragrant wine does not normally give such satisfaction as drinking water when thirsty, nor eating cake as much as having a meal when hungry, nor sleeping on a soft bed as sleeping when tired, things that are in every case more likely for the poor than for the rich.

And are not matters of bodily soundness and all other aspects of good health equally available to the rich and the poor? Surely you could not claim or prove that only the poor get sick while the rich always get a clean bill of health? You find just the opposite, poor people not easily falling victim to incurable ailments whereas on all sides these things develop in the bodies of the rich. Gout, at any rate, hangovers, breakdowns, nervous disorders and all kinds of bad and pernicious discharges usually affect those of high life who smell of perfume, make no effort and take no exercise, and do not have to provide necessary nourishment by working each day. Hence all those living a life of luxury are more wretched even than the mendicants, and not even the well-off themselves would deny it. At least, it has often happened that a rich person lying on his soft bed, with slaves and menials in attendance, enjoying service from them all, has heard a poor person crying out in the alley begging for bread, and has burst into tears and groans, and begged to be like him with his good health rather than have poor health along with wealth.

It is not only in regard to good health but also the rearing of children where you will likewise see the rich no better off than the poor: large families and childlessness affect the one and the other alike (675) – or, rather, you would see in this case also the rich person at a disadvantage. The poor person, you see, if not becoming a father, does not feel much pain, whereas the rich, to the extent that they see their substance increasing, is so much more stung by childlessness, getting no satisfaction from lack of an heir. The poor person's estate, even if he passes on without children, is not worth fighting over on account of its modesty, and it passes on to friends and relatives, whereas the rich person's attracts the eyes of many people from all quarters, and often falls into the hands of his enemies when he dies; if he sees this happening to other people when he is alive, he will live a life more bitter than death, expecting the same thing to happen to him as well.

But do not the circumstances of death affect all in common? does not untimely death befall both rich and poor? do not in all cases after death the bodies of the one and the other dissolve, become dust and ashes, and spawn worms? Yet the circumstances of burial are not common, you say. What difference does it make? After all, when you clothe the rich in much golden finery, you are bringing them nothing other than further resentment and heavier accusation, you are opening everyone's mouths in condemnation of the departed, you are bringing countless curses on them and attaching to them severer criticism of their greed, everyone incensed and outraged and cursing the deceased for not even in death putting an end to their mad lust for possessions. Nor is this the only problem: there is also the fact that this attracts the attention of robbers. And thus greater fuss proves the occasion for greater shame. I mean, while no one would be interested in stripping the body of the poor person, the plainness of the garments proving a protection to the body's attire, in the other case by contrast doors and bars, gates and sentries (676) are all to no purpose, since the lust for possessions encourages those in the habit of such knavery to risk anything. And so the greater display brings on the deceased greater indignity, and whereas the one given a modest burial enjoys respect in peace, the lavish tomb is despoiled and vandalised; should nothing of the kind happen to it, it will still make no difference except to provide a richer banquet for the worms and turn into worse decay. [13]

So, tell me, does this fate deserve to be called blessed? Who is so miserable and wretched as to think a human being enviable on the basis of it? And not this alone: passing on to all the other considerations individually and examining them precisely, we shall find the poor in possession of much more than the rich. Let us consider all this precisely, therefore, and go through it with all the others ("Give a wise person the opportunity," Scripture says, remember, "and they will become wiser"), [14] calling constantly to mind also the fact that not even from the abundance of possessions will anything else accrue to the owners than worries, troubles, fears and dangers. Let us not think we have less than the rich: if we are vigilant, we shall have even more, both in the matters that concern God and in all those of this life. After all, you will find enjoyment and security, a good reputation, health of body, solid spiritual values, sound hope, and not readily sinning among the poor to a greater extent than among the rich.

Let us therefore not grumble in the manner of ungrateful servants nor criticise the Master; rather, let us give thanks for everything, and judge only one thing a disaster, sin, and one thing a good, righteousness. If in fact we are of this disposition, not illness, not poverty, not dishonor, nor any other seeming tribulation will vex us. [15] Instead, by reaping the benefit of unalloyed satisfaction in everything, we shall attain the future goods, thanks to the grace and lovingkindness of our Lord Jesus Christ, to whom with the Father and the Holy Spirit be the glory, for ages of ages. Amen.

Select Bibliography

Barthélemy, D., *Les Devanciers d'Aquila, VTS* X, Leiden, 1963

Baur, P. C., *John Chrysostom and his Time*, 2 vols, Eng. trans., London-Glasgow, 1959,1960

Bouyer, L., *The Spirituality of the New Testament and the Fathers*, Eng. trans., London, 1963

Drewery, B., "Antiochien," *TRE* 3, 103-113

Fernandez Marcos, N., "Some reflections on the Antiochian text of the Septuagint," in D. Fraenkel et al (edd.), *Studien zur Septuaginta – Robert Hanhart zu Ehren*, Göttingen, 1990, 219-229

_____, "The Lucianic text in the Books of Kingdoms," in A. Pietersma et al (edd.), *De Septuaginta*, Mississauga, 1984

_____, *The Septuagint in Context: Introduction to the Greek Versions of the Bible*, Eng. trans., Boston-Leiden, 2001

Hill, R. C., "*Akribeia*: a principle of Chrysostom's exegesis," *Colloquium* 14 (Oct. 1981) 32-36

_____ , "Chrysostom's terminology for the inspired Word," *EstBíb* 41 1983) 367-73

_____ , *St John Chrysostom's Homilies on Genesis*, FOTC 74,82,87, 1986, 1990, 1992

_____ , "Psalm 45: a *locus classicus* for patristic thinking on biblical inspiration," *StudP* 25 (1991) 95-100

_____ , "Chrysostom's Commentary on the Psalms: homilies or tracts?" in P. Allen et al (edd.), *Prayer and Spirituality in the Early Church* I, Brisbane 1998

_____ , "A pelagian commentator on the Psalms?" *ITQ* 65 (1998) 263-71

_____ , *St John Chrysostom. Commentary on the Psalms*, 2 vols, Brookline MA, 1998

_____ , "Chrysostom's homilies on David and Saul," *SVTQ* 44 (2000) 123-41

_____ , "St John Chrysostom's homilies on Hannah," *SVTQ* 45 (2001) 319-38

_____ , "Chrysostom on the obscurity of the Old Testament," *OCP* 67 (2001) 371-83

Kelly, J. N. D., *Early Christian Doctrines*, 5th ed., New York, 1978

_____ , *Golden Mouth. The Story of John Chrysostom. Ascetic, Preacher, Bishop*, Ithaca NY, 1995

Leroux, J.-M., "Johannes Chrysostomus," *TRE* 17, 118-27

Mayer, W., Allen, P., *John Chrysostom*, The Early Church Fathers, London-New York, 2000

van de Paverd, F., *The Homilies on the Statues. An Introduction*, OCA 239, Rome, 1991

Schäublin, C., "Diodor von Tarsus," *TRE* 8, 763-67

_____ , *Untersuchungen zu Methode und Herkunft der Antiochenischen Exegese*, Theophaneia: Beiträge zur Religions- und Kirchengeschichte des Altertums 23, Köln-Bonn, 1974

Ternant, P., "La θεωρία d'Antioche dans le cadre de sens de l''Ecriture," *Bib* 34 (1953) 135-58,354-383,456-86

Vaccari, A., "La θεωρία nella scuola esegetica di Antiochia," *Bib* 1 (1920) 3-36

von Rad, G., *Studies in Deuteronomy*, Studies in Biblical Theology 9, London, 1963

Wallace-Hadrill, D. S., *Christian Antioch. A Study of Early Christian Thought in the East*, Cambridge, 1982

Young, F., *Biblical Exegesis and the Formation of Christian Culture*, Cambridge, 1997

NOTES

Notes to Introduction
¹ For a more extensive study of these homilies, cf my article, "Chrysostom's homilies on David and Saul." In 1898 a translation of the David and Saul homilies into Russian was made, and an English version of this Russian text by Isaac E. Lambertsen appears in *Living Orthodoxy* 19 (1998) 11-32.

Notes to Homilies on David and Saul
Homily One
¹ Like any good pedagogue, Chrysostom begins with a practical example from his listeners' experience. The text of these three homilies occurs in PG 54.675-707, from the eighteenth century edition of Bernard de Montfaucon; no modern critical edition has appeared.

² For the historical setting of these homilies, and the connection with homilies given earlier in this year 387, see Introduction.

³ Chrysostom is evidently referring either to his homily on that parable (PG 51.17-30) or to his summary of it in the twentieth homily on the Statues, delivered late in Lent, after the torture of the miscreants and not long before Bishop Flavian's return from his journey to Constantinople to intercede with the Emperor. There, as he had in the third homily, Chrysostom cites Matthew's parable (18.23-35) of the Unmerciful Servant – or, rather, the Merciful Master – as basis of a plea for the Emperor's forgiveness. Before closing, he also touches on one pervading theme of the Statues series, avoidance of oaths.

⁴ Is Chrysostom cutely divining his own shortcomings? He would not seem to be too wide of the mark. Gentleness is the particular virtue with which Chrysostom credits David (and Moses) in commenting on Pss 45; 132. Is this, however, a different theme, or is he reinforcing the point of that earlier homily for the benefit of the court?

⁵ The fact that the exemplar of clemency is of royal rank would also influence the choice if the Emperor's clemency was recently an issue (a factor editor Montfaucon does not envisage).

⁶ Acts 13.22; cf 1 Sam 13.14; Ps 89.20.

⁷ In his commentary on Ps 7.4, Chrysostom remarked at length on David's surpassing the talion law, which Jesus cites in Matt 5.38 only to depart from it, as had the rabbis, thinking it too harsh (despite its formulation in Deut 19.21 "to restrict indiscriminate vendetta by applying

135

a rough principle of equity," as Joseph Blenkinsopp remarks).

[8] Is Chrysostom referring to a previous homily? That twentieth homily (or the twenty first, relaying Bishop Flavian's appeal to the Emperor) on the Statues does not cite David and Saul.

[9] 1 Sam 17.33.

[10] 1 Sam 17.32 LXX.

[11] 1 Sam 18.6-8 in the local form of the LXX, which reveals some individual features. (I have examined this Antiochene form of the LXX elsewhere, e.g., in the introduction to my translation of Chrysostom's Commentary on the Psalms).

[12] Preachers the world over, of course, profess not to develop points they then proceed to develop at greater length; Chrysostom's *makrologia* is notorious.

[13] A conflation of 1 Sam 18.14,16,20; 19.1 in the local form of the LXX.

[14] 1 Sam 18.10-11.

[15] 1 Sam 18.25.

[16] 1 Sam 18.23. It is narrative only (in support of his theme) that Chrysostom is interested in, not details of the text examined in Antiochene fashion.

[17] 1 Sam 19.10.

[18] Chrysostom has been rehearsing the narrative of Saul's ingratitude to David, almost as though he has forgotten his theme and the contemporary situation to which the narrative applies. But he pauses – still without adverting explicitly to recent events in Antioch – to present David as surpassing the requirements of the talion law, as he had done earlier (see note 7), and thus proving a model for royal forbearance. And he proceeds to explicate the moral involved, as though interested ears in the palace were listening.

[19] 1 Sam 24.3-6. The narrative is gripping enough, but the preacher embellishes it with his own figurative and even allegorical representation of the scene. Then his focus shifts to David's henchmen and the pressure they exert on him – as if the emperor is coming under similar pressure from his advisers on the Antioch troubles and is in danger of succumbing? Chrysostom thus cannot afford to leave David alone in the cave, as he does in telling this incident (or the similar one in 1 Sam 26) in Homily Two on Hannah, where no such theme of forbearance is being labored. Does this suggest the Hannah homilies preceded these? The preacher, of course, is capable of altering details of the text to suit the occasion.

[20] We are probably not in a position to know how closely this weighing up of pros and cons in the struggle to save a life corresponded in detail to the contemporary developments in Antioch and Constantinople.

[21] In his analysis of this biblical incident Chrysostom is doing everything but blatantly say to Constantinople: pay no heed to advisers who highlight the risk involved in pardoning a miscreant populace that may offend again.

[22] In terms not dissimilar to his account of Flavian's appeal to the Emperor in Homily 21 on the Statues, Chrysostom develops his theme,

"the quality of mercy is not strained," even claiming that forbearance makes one angelic – a claim that as an Antiochene he has to temper somewhat.

²³ Rom 13.2.

²⁴ 1 Sam 20.27. Chrysostom's laboring this point of maintaining a level of respect and formality in language can perhaps be seen corresponding to his criticism of the use of oaths, a theme of those Lenten homilies. Has the homily's predominant theme, forbearance, been disposed of?

²⁵ Has Chrysostom, after examining in detail the incident recorded in ch 24 of 1 Sam of Saul entering the cave where David and his men were hiding, now repeated the mistake made in the second homily on Hannah of confusing it with its doublet in ch 26, where David comes across the sleeping Saul? As in that Hannah homily, he also uses the strange expression "double (διπλοῦς) cave" as though incorrectly recalling διπλοίς, "cloak." This conclusion to the homily has some other features which suggest a different treatment, a different stenographer, or even a different author. In fact, the homily as a whole shows fewer signs of orality than the Hannah homilies – though we have admitted in the Introduction that spontaneity is something that can depend on the manner of recording of the homily.

²⁶ Because, as suggested in the previous note, the text of this homily does not betray features of the context of delivery, we have not before had grounds for drawing conclusions about the composition of the congregation. This remark of his would suggest men only were present, or at least in the preacher's thinking. He also refers below to "noble men (ἄνδρες)" alone in the Scriptures – just as he presented Hannah as a rare exception. As elsewhere in his preaching, Chrysostom envisages the Christian household as a little Bible group ruminating on key texts.

²⁷ As also emerged in his treatment of the Hannah story, Chrysostom thinks of the Scriptures primarily as hagiographical and moral, offering a range of salutary models for all walks of life.

Homily Two

¹ Just as Chrysostom had spoken in the first homily of this series of the interval since the twentieth homily on the Statues as "the other day," πρώ ην, so he uses the term again.

² Rom 1.32-2.1.

³ Gen 12.3.

⁴ 1 Sam 24.7 (from the first of the doublets of this episode; cf note 25 on the previous homily). We have noted that Chrysostom refers to this biblical author not as προφήτης but as συγγραφεύς.

⁵ As an Antiochene Chrysostom is always ready to balance divine grace with the character's human contribution. Cf note 14 below.

⁶ In eulogising David's feat, Chrysostom wants to present him as a liturgical leader – first, a priest (in Old Testament terms, ἱερεύς, appropriately), then (in New Testament terms) an ἐπίσκοπος, bishop or priest, then victim (ἱερεῖον) and ἱερεύς again. Is there in all this a further appeal to the emperor, called to be a priestly David?

⁷ 1 Sam 24.8.

⁸ Chrysostom is just the one with the gifts to dramatise this incident and highlight the value of stemming royal resentment – precisely what the current situation at Antioch and Constantinople required.

⁹ The incident of the three young men in the furnace in Dan 3 is much beloved by Chrysostom and his contemporaries as examples of the righteous sufferer.

¹⁰ Chrysostom reverts now (unwittingly) to the other version of this incident, in 1 Sam 26, where Saul is asleep.

¹¹ The practical benefits of sparing wrongdoers are now adduced to strengthen Chrysostom's case.

¹² Is the intended listener a member of the congregation, or the emperor in Constantinople? Self-interest is still the line Chrysostom is taking.

¹³ 1 Sam 24.8.

¹⁴ Not exactly in keeping with normal Antiochene thinking on the balance between σπουδή and χάρις. Cf note 5 above.

¹⁵ Cf 1 Sam 18.9,29. Though in the case of other parts of the Bible, such as Genesis and the Psalms, Chrysostom can speak of the orality of the inspired Word and the authors as προφῆται, we have noted that in the case of the Former Prophets the author is termed a συγγραφεύς responsible for "writing a book."

¹⁶ Gal 5.10. Both the perceptive example from family life and the New Testament parallel help the congregation grasp the point – as well as allow the preacher to rationalise an apparent contradiction in the text.

¹⁷ 1 Sam 24.10. Was the court meant to understand by this that Antioch was getting bad press, and would prefer to stand on its otherwise good record?

¹⁸ Again some cogent examples from real life.

¹⁹ 1 Sam 24.11. Are we to judge, from the emphasis laid on this talisman, that some similar pledge was produced at court to testify to Antioch's good faith?

²⁰ Cf 1 Sam 24.11 LXX. Again there is an implication that a previous good record could be cited – on David's part and Antioch's.

²¹ 1 Sam 17.33.

²² 1 Sam 24.13. David's appeal to a higher court, of course, was not without relevance to the current situation, nor to the way Bishop Flavian conducted his intercession if Homily 21 on the Statues is to be believed.

²³ Cf 2 Sam 1.21 in the local form of the LXX. The fact that Jonathan fell in the same battle is given less attention by Chrysostom than it might.

²⁴ 2 Sam 1.23.

²⁵ Has Chrysostom reduced the congregation to tears? or is this mere rhetorical exaggeration? or simply a manufactured 'appearance of actuality,' in Dom Baur's term? The fact that he has left any moralising to this brief conclusion would confirm the impression that his purpose in these homilies is to apply the story of David's forbearance to a different situation, like the appeal currently being made to the emperor.

[26] The occupant of the throne at Constantinople could hardly avoid the thrust of this remark; the parenesis applies more closely there than to his listeners on the day. The fact that the message, though consistent and even unremitting, is not blatant confirms the impression that it was in fact intended for royal consumption at the time; the preacher (perhaps uncharacteristically) keeps a grip on himself, there being much at stake.

Homily Three

[1] Irregular attendance by members of his congregation irks Chrysostom, like many a preacher; the homilies on Hannah gave ample evidence of that. When people absented themselves to attend spectacles, like the racetrack (more than horseracing being involved, it emerges from Chrysostom's Homily 6 on Genesis) or the theatre, he is especially upset.

[2] This is a clear indication that the occasion of at least this homily was a liturgical and indeed eucharistic one; publicly acknowledged sinners were not welcome at such assemblies. Chrysostom reveals the discipline of the sacraments in his church: in the absence of a specific sacrament of private reconciliation (Confession: see note 5), and yet not going the way of Novatian rigorism in denying the possibility of forgiveness of serious sin after baptism (*the* sacrament of forgiveness), his church excluded sinners on a temporary basis provided they repented – something not true of the phantom theatre-goers.

[3] Matt 5.28.

[4] From experience or hearsay Chrysostom is able to give a devastating picture of the unsavoury character of the theatre, and leave no grounds for thinking anyone came away uncontaminated. Kelly (we shall see in connection with the very first homily on Hannah) reported on the reputation of the citizens of Antioch for pleasure-seeking, including attendance at the theatre. It is men Chrysostom is addressing, of course – there being no women in the congregation? What follows would suggest as much.

[5] To render this term ἐξομολόγησις as simply "confession" could give the impression that Chrysostom's church knew the ritual of private reconciliation that later developed in the West, as distinct from what Kelly describes as "a prescribed course of self-humiliation and prostration known technically as *exomologesis*." It was not to be taken advantage of frequently, a practice Chrysostom was accused of having promoted, we are told by the historian of Constantinople, Socrates.

[6] The rhetoric of the delivery reflects the preacher's disgust at the attendance of these depraved entertainments by some members of his congregation assembled for liturgy of Word and eucharist.

[7] It has been a lengthy digression, the Statues aftermath paling into insignificance by comparison with the listeners' lapses. We should note, however, that this opening to the homily bears a close resemblance to a homily of Pseudo-Chrysostom (numbered 4563 by M. Geerard in the *Clavis* II to CCG.)

[8] Though the ordinary reader of the Former Prophets would not get

the strongest impression of David's gentleness, πραότης, for the purposes of this series of homilies it is given particular emphasis, and this virtue remains in Chrysostom's mind in other of his works, such as the Psalms Commentary (if, in fact, that work has not preceded them).

⁹ Back into focus comes the parable of the Unmerciful Servant, or Merciful Master (Matt 18.23-35), cited at the opening of these homilies in the wake of the third and twentieth homilies on the Statues as the paradigm of forbearance.

¹⁰ Cf Matt 6.14.

¹¹ We are back on track, delivering a message to the court, though the biblical text has not much more to offer, the preacher simply trying to extract still more from the same story.

¹² Forbearance is a matter of self-interest: a message for the emperor (as developed in the speech of Flavian, as Chrysostom recounts it in Homily 21 on the Statues) as also for the congregation, to whom finally he is applying the biblical story.

¹³ Cf 1 Cor 15.31, loosely recalled.

¹⁴ Matt 5.11-12.

¹⁵ Luke 6.22-23, loosely recalled.

¹⁶ Luke 18.11 loosely recalled.

¹⁷ Luke 18.14.

¹⁸ We have observed that Chrysostom, now halfway through the homily, has not taken his study of the biblical David story further, choosing to tease out for his congregation's benefit some of the moral implications of that and other biblical examples, such as the parables. The interval between second and third homilies he speaks of again as πρώην, possibly in the sense of "the day before yesterday."

¹⁹ 1 Sam 24.16.

²⁰ Having made his point to the palace, Chrysostom is able to revert to his customary expansiveness and his use of telling examples from nature to develop his parenesis. He may also be suggesting, however, that the emperor has been under a misapprehension about the character of the people of Antioch.

²¹ 1 Sam 17.45, Chrysostom loosely recalling the first clause, or reading a quite different version.

²² Cf Josh 10.12-13.

²³ Cf Exod 14.21,26.

²⁴ Cf Dan 3.24,50 LXX.

²⁵ David's words in 1 Sam 24.9, but not quite in this form nor in reply to Saul's question.

²⁶ Cf Rom 12.10. The moral application Chrysostom proceeds to make (which admittedly has possible relevance to the current situation) seems trivial, but reflecting something of his own sensitivity demonstrated throughout his ministry.

²⁷ Phil 2.3.

²⁸ Prov 25.15; 15.1.

[29] Ben Sira, in fact (Sir 28.12) – another sage, but not quite the previous one quoted. Chrysostom appreciates a good analogy when he sees one.

[30] 1 Sam 24.17, the text not quite expressing Saul's remorse in such strong terms.

[31] Chrysostom appears to be going to great lengths to apply the moral (which biographers suggest he might also have learnt himself) to his congregation; but it is possible the palace was also meant to hear it (as it also matches the argumentation of Flavian in the twenty first homily on the Statues).

[32] 1 Sam 24.18.

[33] 1 Sam 24.19.

[34] 1 Sam 24.20-21.

[35] Chrysostom is referring to Mephibosheth, whose story is somewhat slanted to support the general message to the palace of forbearance: the ἔκγονος of Saul is in fact the son of Jonathan – hence David's interest in him; he was no "child," having a son of his own at the time of this incident narrated in 2 Sam 9 (well after Saul's death, in fact, narrated in 1 Sam 31); his later complicity in Absalom's rebellion is suppressed, as it would have sent a wrong message to the court, whereas by Theodoret this character is frequently referred to as proverbial for treachery.

[36] Matt 6.14 loosely recalled.

Notes to Homilies on Hannah

[1] For a more extensive study of these homilies, cf my article "St John Chrysostom's homilies on Hannah."

Homily One

[1] The timing of these homilies around Pentecost of the year 387 is discussed in the Introduction. The text of the five homilies appears in PG 54.631-676; no modern critical edition has been prepared.

[2] Chrysostom's preaching of (even less palatable) spiritual truths is always enlivened by the use of effective and sustained metaphors.

[3] The assemblies (σύλλογοι, συνάξεις), not necessarily liturgical, on the days of Lent proved occasions for fruitful experience of the ministry of the word. Chrysostom's (extant) homilies on Genesis, for example, were delivered during such Lenten assemblies (Genesis being the text for that period of the liturgical year); see Introduction to my translation of the Genesis homilies.

[4] No one could say the preacher was not in contact with real living conditions in Antioch.

[5] Another effective figure. Does the nature of it suggest that only men were present in "this church" before "this altar"? (Chrysostom's Psalms Commentary was delivered instead in a διδασκαλεῖον, men only being present again, the text suggests; see Introduction to my translation.) Drunkenness was in his sights in the first homily before Lent this year, the

baleful events that followed serving to document it.

⁶ The events that followed the desecration of the imperial statues, including Bishop Flavian's successful journey to Constantinople to appeal for clemency and his triumphal return at Easter, and developments in the wake of that crisis (of which Chrysostom treated in the Lenten homilies on the Statues), are recounted in the Introduction.

⁷ Is Chrysostom here summarising his discourse to the pagans, or (as he promised above) giving a synopsis of his Lenten homilies to remind his congregation of the advantages of fasting? Editor Montfaucon's subheading suggests the former, but the text the latter – though this summary is much more orderly than the material in homilies (on the Statues – e.g., nos. 7 to 9) delivered during that fear-filled Lent.

⁸ Discernment, θεωρία, is a key notion for an Antiochene theologian – the ability to get beyond the surface, whether (as here) in the case of created things, or in reading the Scriptures to find the true meaning. (The word is also used in Homily Four for the spectacle that some of Chrysostom's congregation found so fascinating at the racecourse.)

⁹ Ps 104.24. Acknowledgement of the transcendence of the Creator is, of course, basic to Eastern thought.

¹⁰ This is a key term in Chrysostom's theology of the oikonomia: ἀσθέ νεια, the limitations (or weakness) of created things, including human beings. It has a positive value in that it invites divine considerateness, συνκατάβασις.

¹¹ For Chrysostom the endemic flaw in human nature is indifference, ῥᾳθυμία, the cause of the Fall of the first parents.

¹² This is turning into a carefully crafted and embellished summary of the Lenten preaching on creation (Genesis traditionally supplying the readings for that season). Perhaps the preacher is allowing for the possibility that some of his listeners were not present for (all) the Lenten homilies – or taking the opportunity to gild the lily. In the course of it, his readiness to rationalise emerges in the face of any difficulty proposed.

¹³ The verb Chrysostom uses of conscience inspiring the human being (ἐνηχεῖν) he uses also for the divine inspiration of the biblical authors.

¹⁴ After the lengthy introduction, that has served various purposes, including the connection with the Lenten sermons (six weeks in the past), Chrysostom is finally – if obliquely – moving in the direction of the subject of these homilies, Hannah, though he begins here by referring (literally) to "the *father* assigned to each of us."

¹⁵ 1 Tim 2.14-15, a text that betrays the literalist interpretation of Genesis of both author of the Pastorals and Chrysostom, and at least in our day is hardly a winning introduction to the topic of women's role in the rearing of children.

¹⁶ 1 Tim 5.10. Chrysostom gives the impression that in his time it was not taken for granted that education of the children fell as much to mothers as to fathers. In fact, the language of this section on parenthood has (in the original) been largely masculine, posing a quandary for a translator as to

whether this has been deliberately exclusive (especially in view of the composition of the congregation) or simply conventional. In the light of these later remarks, the former is suggested – hence the need for particular reference to women (were any present?).

[17] Cf 1 Sam 1.2, where the text does not confirm Peninnah's "many" children – but it helps the story. Is Chrysostom citing here the real reason for his choosing the Former Prophets and Hannah in particular as the subject of treatment? We shall find that as the series of homilies goes on, the preacher has doubts about the mileage he can extract from the topic and the direction he should give to it – doubts perhaps reflected in the poor attendance he will lament.

[18] Peninnah's scorn for the childless Hannah is an item (not in our Hebrew text but) only in the Antiochene form of the Septuagint (styled by some in antiquity as "Lucianic," as also by some modern scholars), occurring probably under the influence of Hagar's scorn for the childless Sarai in Gen 16.5. (For information on the form of the LXX used by Chrysostom and other Antiochenes, see Introduction to my translation of his *Commentary on the Psalms*.)

[19] 1 Sam 1.6 LXX.

[20] 1 Sam 1.7 LXX.

[21] Chrysostom's biographer Kelly may have grounds for speaking of Chrysostom's "scorn and also disparagement of the female sex;" but in this instance he shows he is capable of achieving greater balance in his attitude to the sexes, especially if men only are present for this homily.

[22] For Chrysostom all the Old Testament authors are προφῆται, but he can make an exception for the Former Prophets; so he speaks here of the author as "συγγραφεύς." (See my "Chrysostom's terminology for the inspired Word.")

[23] Cf 1 Sam 1.5,8.

[24] 1 Sam 1.9. Later in life, during his exile, Chrysostom will show a like impatience with the depression, ἀθυμία, of his loyal correspondent Olympias in his letters to her.

[25] This typical index of Antiochene precision, ἀκρίβεια, is recurring like a refrain: "not without purpose." Even a miniscule item of expression by the biblical author is found to have significance for the commentator, whose precision (not "accuracy," as often rendered: we have seen Chrysostom inaccurately reproducing the biblical text, e.g.) must match that of the biblical author. (See my "*Akribeia*: a principle of Chrysostom's exegesis.")

[26] The audience could not but be moved by these sustained similes.

[27] 1 Sam 1.11. Whereas our Hebrew text reads only *Yahweh Sabaoth*, Chrysostom's text seems to provide three divine names: one is in Greek (despite his comment), and he chooses not to give a version of the others. (Hebrew, we know, was not his strong suit.)

[28] Another telling figure, perhaps influenced by Ps 45.1, which Chrysostom (like many other Fathers) uses to develop his thinking on biblical inspiration. (See my "Psalm 45: a *locus classicus* for patristic thinking

on biblical inspiration.")

[29] Men do not behave in this fashion, of course.

[30] Or "man" (ἄνθρωπος for ἀνήρ, an imprecision Chrysostom can be guilty of): men can learn from this woman.

[31] Cf 1 Sam 1.20.

[32] Though Chrysostom begins by an appeal to both women and men to take the example of Hannah and look after the children, it soon becomes clear that young males and married men are principally in focus – not surprising if the congregation is exclusively male.

[33] We noted at the outset of this homily (see note 4) that Chrysostom gives the impression of being a keen observer of contemporary morals (unless he is simply recycling traditional material on male promiscuity).

[34] An alternative reading incorporates a negative into this clause.

Homily Two

[1] The adverb πρώην (repeated below) can more precisely stipulate "the day before yesterday." Editor Montfaucon, however, would see this homily being preached on the Saturday after the Ascension (the feast falling on June 9 that year 387) after the first homily two days before the feast.

[2] Ps 126.5.

[3] 1 Sam 1.7. We might think the preacher had already brought out the pain of childlessness, and that to return to the theme with Homeric similes is to gild the lily somewhat – the *makrologia* for which Chrysostom gained a reputation.

[4] Just a brief reminder to the congregation of the correlative elements in spiritual growth according to the Antiochene tenets of spirituality – human effort and divine grace.

[5] Even Homer might blanch at sustaining the metaphor to this extent and beyond.

[6] 1 Sam 2.5, from the song of Hannah extolling the paradoxes in God's dealings with people (an inspiration for the Lukan Magnificat). Chrysostom – perversely? – prefers, for his fiscal metaphor, to take it as historical statement of Hannah's family, though he knows from 2.21 that Hannah had only five more children, boys and girls. He evidently thought it not the moment to discourse on the significance of the number seven.

[7] Another slight to any women present for this homily (he had spoken above of "the women among us," though not necessarily implying presence at that time).

[8] 1 Sam 1.12. In v.14 the LXX speaks of a "boy," παιδάριον ("minister," *puer* in the Latin of Erasmus), who does the chiding for the priest.

[9] With typical Antiochene precision, Chrysostom conducts his commentary by picking up items in the text and establishing that they are "not without purpose" (cf note 25 on the previous homily).

[10] 1 Sam 1.11.

[11] Matt 6.7.

[12] Luke 18.1-5, the preacher gilding the lily again to present the judge

as "cruel and inhumane" in addition to his being proof against influence of any kind.

[13] Rom 12.12; 1 Thess 5.17.

[14] Prayer for Chrysostom and his school is something for which there are rules that can be followed, as he reveals also in his Commentary on the Psalms (e.g., Pss 4;7); the spiritual director has less to say about communion with God. In the words of Louis Bouyer, it is an "asceticism without mysticism."

[15] Exod 14.15.

[16] 1 Sam 1.14 LXX, Eli himself the speaker in the Hebrew (likewise the Vulgate), no mention of a παιδάριον. Chrysostom, predictably, will make capital out of this additional textual item.

[17] Cf 2 Sam 16.5-13. Absalom and Shimei are among Chrysostom's favorite examples for establishing David as a model of the righteous sufferer and a paradigm of meekness, appearing frequently in this role in his Commentary on the Psalms (e.g. Ps 45.4).

[18] Cf 2 Sam 16.10,12.

[19] This story in 1 Sam 24 is a doublet of that in ch 26, commentators tell us, and involves a number of difficulties in sequence (which Chrysostom augments by excluding the men from the cave to gild the lily again). Does his reference to the "double wall" (διπλοῦν τειχίον) come from a hasty reading of διπλοΐς, the cloak in which Saul is wrapped and a corner of which David does in fact take? Saul and this incident, incidentally, also figure in that commentary on Ps 45.4 to document further David's meekness (relevant here?), as in Homily 1 on David and Saul below.

[20] Sir 23.18.

[21] Cf 1 Sam 24.11. The thought is departing from its original direction somewhat: Hannah exemplified immunity to slights even in her depression, a theme which David also documented; but the latter's respect for Saul's position has been cited to illustrate a different thought, the need to respect priests (even more than kings). Longwinded preachers are liable to stray from the point.

[22] Matt 23.2-3.

[23] Matt 10.41.

[24] Chrysostom is aware he has gone off on a number of digressions – but he is not finished yet, bringing the story of Job, another of the righteous sufferers, and his wife (and a further reference to David and Shimei) into play.

[25] Job 2.10.

[26] "In manly fashion," literally.

[27] A commendable stance in a commentator.

[28] Chrysostom seems to be suggesting that the drinking habits of the clergy (as today) were the subject of comment, justified or not – which may explain his opening reference to the subject in the first homily above, as it formed the subject matter also of the first of the homilies on the Statues before the fatal incident.

[28] It is interesting to observe that Chrysostom adopted a different approach in that first homily on the Statues to people found uttering

blasphemies: if his listeners asked them to desist and they did not, falling to blows was the necessary recourse (John the Baptist, not Hannah, the model adduced).

[29] For a preacher on inebriation and related social habits, Chrysostom seems to have a close knowledge of his subject.

[30] 1 Sam 1.15.

[31] 1 Sam 1.16 in Chrysostom's form of the LXX.

[32] Cf Rom 12.17.

[33] 1 Sam 1.17.

[34] 1 Sam 1.18.

Homily Three

[1] Again Chrysostom uses πρώην without necessarily indicating this homily was given on the day after the previous one. Montfaucon places it three days later, on Tuesday of the week after the Ascension, June 14.

[2] An apparently careless conflation of vv.8-12 and 28 of 1 Cor 12.

[3] Rom 12.15.

[4] Are we to presume from the contrast drawn with Hannah that Chrysostom is addressing women in his congregation (in this homily), even if he proceeds to indicate that the problems for which help should be sought are not principally gynecological?

[5] Jer 23.23.

[6] For Chrysostom ῥαθυμία is the capital sin.

[7] 1 Cor 10.11. As emerges often from his biblical commentaries, for Chrysostom Scripture's character and purpose are primarily hagiographical and moral – a predictable stance in a homilist.

[8] 1 Sam 1.23.

[9] Cf 1 Sam 1.22.

[10] An effective preacher is always tempted to embellish an austere text from a human point of view so as to affect his audience more potently. The pathos of this relationship, however, is not the focus of this biblical author, whose more dogmatic intentions center on Samuel's role in offsetting the shortcomings of Eli and his sons, Hannah disappearing from view in ch 2.

[11] Is the succession of images getting out of hand? The young Samuel is presumably the lamb and the calf: is he also the fragrant flower with lasting fragrance? It was Hannah who was described in these terms at the homily's opening.

[12] Ps 1.1-3, where the exclusive language in Hebrew and LXX is not equally applicable to both mother and son.

[13] 1 Sam 1.24 LXX. Chrysostom continues to dramatize the incident, putting the congregation in Hannah's shoes.

[14] Such comments would doubtless be appreciated by those anxious to promote the cause of women's ministry. Hannah turns priestess, "ἱέρεια," her sacrifice is better than that of the "ἱερεύς," and in fact rivals that of Abraham for completeness, Chrysostom adding that gender is no bar to

the essence of priesthood (at least internally, where Hannah and Abraham both excelled) – in Shiloh, if not in Antioch.

[15] 1 Sam 1.26-28.

[16] Matt 6.21.

[17] 1 Sam 2.20. Chrysostom seems not to take the sexist cue of the author in transferring credit to the father.

[18] Cf Gen 3.16. In his enthusiastic encomium of Hannah, Chrysostom is even prepared to see her cancelling the curse of Eve, where a more Marian commentator would think this role already spoken for.

[19] Only if no women were present in the congregation would this statement not give rise to false expectations, surely.

[20] A muddled conflation of vv.15,19 of 1 Cor 6, followed by 2 Cor 6.16.

[21] Hag 1.4.

[22] Matt 21.13 citing Isa 56.7; Jer 7.11.

[23] Chrysostom's attention to Hannah (who, admittedly, has been lost from sight in this rather rambling homily) is all the more noteworthy when one considers the society of the time that placed women among other marginalized groups.

[24] Titus 1.16; 1 Tim 5.8; Col 3.5. Antiochene spirituality, of course, required this balance of faith and works, the balance tipping often in favor of the latter.

Homily Four

[1] On the grounds of Chrysostom's statement below that he had spoken lately on the first part of the prayer (1 Sam 2.1a), Montfaucon judges that a homily (delivered on June 16) has been lost; the final homily also speaks of two whole διαλέξεις being devoted to Hannah's prayer. So this is in effect the fifth homily in the series, delivered two days later, Pentecost eve (as emerges later in this homily) – though below, to make a point, Chrysostom claims the συνάξεις are held only once on the day.

[2] Unlike many a preacher, Chrysostom admits (notionally) it is not fair to chastise those present for the sins of the absent. Is the occasion eucharistic? He mentions readings from προφῆται and ἀπόστολοι, and sees a slight delivered also to πατέρες (clergy present?).

[3] Jer 3.6, though it is Israel who is in fact mentioned in the text.

[4] Throughout his life Chrysostom showed himself sensitive to slights, his ill-considered response often landing him in difficulties. In this case his pique at the defection of many of his congregation leads to a digression half the length of the homily proper – poor judgement, surely.

[5] The capital sin ῥᾳθυμία is again is the cause of irregular attendance.

[6] Chrysostom forecasts a mass exodus to the races on day after Pentecost; and as in his Homily 6 on Genesis, where he is even more upset at the congregation's attendance at the races, he implies that racecourses were the scene of more than simply the sport of kings. Kelly observes: "The citizens of Antioch had a reputation for pleasure-seeking, worldliness, fickleness and cynicism; among other diversions they had a passion for

horse-racing and the theater, and in spring and summer they streamed out to Daphne for relaxation and amusement."

[7] In that Homily 6 on Genesis, Chrysostom cites the identical claims of his congregation about conditions in church (adding that the church's ceiling is sufficient distraction from them – an attribute not true of this church, apparently), which he likewise refutes by their willingness to accept worse conditions at the races.

[8] Is Chrysostom detailing the elements of a eucharistic liturgy, or a non-eucharistic synaxis? As Pentecost is to be celebrated next day, the former is unlikely (though cf Homily Five).

[9] 2 Tim 2.22.

[10] Sir 25.24,19.

[11] 1 Tim 2.14.

[12] Chrysostom, with the sages and Paul of the Pastorals as his mentors, with whose literalist exegesis of Gen 3 he concurs, has no warm esteem for women (Kelly brands him "an incorrigible sexist"). To him Hannah is proving an exception rather than the rule he finds formulated in Scripture and vindicated in general practice. (Were women present to hear this back-handed compliment?) He never could resist criticizing their apparel and make-up.

[13] 1 Sam 2.1. It is on the basis of Chrysostom's claim here to have commented on the former clause "the other day" that editor Montfaucon presumes a homily (the fourth, delivered on June 16, two days previously) has been lost. Further confirmation of the loss comes from the statement in the next homily that two whole homilies were devoted to Hannah's prayer.

[14] Apparently loose recall of Ps 75.10 and 1 Sam 2.10, unless Chrysostom's form of the LXX reads this way (Ps 75 missing from his Psalms Commentary).

[15] Cf Isa 40.6-8.

[16] Nothing raises Chrysostom's ire more than the futile efforts of the rich and famous to guarantee their memory with vulgar displays of funerary magnificence, as emerges from his commentary on Ps 49.

[17] The preacher from Antioch, whose experience of life beyond its region was limited, and who could berate his listeners for their own lack of familiarity with biblical figures, is drawing the long bow here to depict Hannah, a woman, as on everyone's lips – all to make a moral point, surely; Antiochene ἀκρίβεια did not forbid this, evidently. It could be that he is finding the biblical text on this story not quite adequate for a series of homilies, and so he is forced to have recourse to hyperbole and digression.

[18] Dan 3, a favorite locus of Chrysostom's for documenting the theme of the righteous sufferer.

[19] Ps 63.1. The commentary is progressing by the Antiochene procedure of ἀκρίβεια, picking up miniscule elements of the text to find significance in them, and then look for a scriptural parallel.

[20] Ps 22.1.

[21] Ps 91.2.

²² Exod 3.6, the import of which is to stress Moses' authentic introduction to the God of the patriarchs, not to bring out God's relationship with individuals. But, as we observed in note 17, in the case of a preacher like Chrysostom, everything serves the purpose in hand – or as the Italian saw has it, *se non è vero, ben trovato.*

²³ Heb 11.16,13.

²⁴ A conflation of vv.14-16 and 10 of Heb 11.

²⁵ Like many a preacher since his time, Chrysostom can come out with other-worldly sentiments that are less than helpful for his congregation living in the world.

²⁶ Ps 119.164. As his Commentary on the Psalms also demonstrates, Chrysostom does not aspire to lead his listeners to deep mystical experience, but he has some tips to give about praying. See my "The spirituality of Chrysostom's Commentary on the Psalms."

²⁷ Though Hannah is (supposed to be) the model of prayer in this homily, the language here is exclusively male, a viewpoint heightened by this example and some further ones.

²⁸ 1 Sam 1.13,19 loosely recalled. As note 17 suggests, Chrysostom is not finding Hannah's prayer as fertile a text as it promised, and he has abandoned it for a wide-ranging lecture on prayer, dealing also with the situation of men caught up in legal business. If he is preaching in the Old Church (not the Great Church: cf note 7 above), close to the agora of Antioch, this example has particular relevance.

²⁹ We get the impression Chrysostom is giving his listeners a mantra to recite, which would be in keeping with his somewhat mechanical approach to prayer.

³⁰ Chrysostom (here and below in connection with the brigand crucified with Jesus) speaks of a εὐκτήριος οἶκος, as also elsewhere in his works when referring (not to a church but) to an oratory such as a martyr's chapel (of which Antioch boasted several) and the classroom, διδασκαλεῖον, in which he delivered his Commentary on the Psalms (see the Introduction to my translation).

³¹ Cf Acts 16.23-33.

³² Cf 2 Kgs 20.1-6.

³³ Hannah aside, the Scriptures do not offer many examples of women's virtue; so Chrysostom can perhaps be excused for confining his attention to ἄνδρες (though his male-oriented viewpoint emerges in his use above of ἄνθρωπος for a man by contrast with the woman praying at the loom).

³⁴ Cf Luke 23.40-43.

³⁵ Cf Jer 38. Chrysostom seems to have forgotten he is adducing examples of wicked men; cf note 22.

³⁶ Cf Dan 6.

³⁷ Cf Jonah 1.17.

³⁸ Again this preacher from Antioch offers his listeners guidance as to practicalities of prayer rather than its more mystical aspects.

Homily Five

¹ Cf note 1 to the previous homily for reasons for supposing it is the fifth in the series, the (fourth) homily delivered three days before Pentecost having been lost. The present homily was clearly delivered after Pentecost; in seeming to suggest he had made much use of the parable of the Merciful Father and Prodigal Son (Luke 15.11-32) in the preceding one (a parable not cited in our text), is Chrysostom also giving us reason to think a further homily has gone missing? Or was another sermon – not referring to Hannah – directed, perhaps on the day of Pentecost itself or shortly after, at recent absentees? (Montfaucon, who is not precise about the day after Pentecost when the final extant homily was delivered, raises no such issue.)

² Cf Luke 15.31, the remark passed by the father to the elder, ever-present brother.

³ Matt 18.20. Chrysostom proceeds to itemize the elements of the day's liturgy, not mentioning – at this point, unlike below – the eucharistic rite (out of reverence?).

⁴ This time Chrysostom seems to refer to the day's synaxis as eucharistic, though – predictably – it is the instruction given by the preacher (who is not the eucharistic celebrant?) that is at the focus of his attention. He was not always given a fair hearing, it seems, especially on the big feast-days with the larger, less fervent, congregations.

⁵ Editor Montfaucon (PG 53.21; 54.632) explains that, despite earlier references to Pentecost in manuscripts and previous editions of these homilies, editors Fronto de Duc and Savile read Μεσοπεντηκοστή at this point, without support from the manuscripts to which Montfaucon has access or the overall sense (Mesopentecost being a festal period before the Ascension). He therefore concludes it is a copyist's error for Πεντηκοστή.

⁶ This is a fair statement of the key principle of Antiochene exegesis/commentary: ἀκρίβεια, precision, in the text requires a like ἀκρίβεια in the exegete, picking up every textual detail (see my "*Akribeia*: a principle of Chrysostom's exegesis"). This principle, however, does not adequately account for Chrysostom's lack of progress beyond this verse in the previous homilies, as he would like us to believe. See notes 17 and 28 on the previous homily.

⁷ 1 Sam 2.1.

⁸ Rom 8.39-40.

⁹ Col 1.24; Rom 5.3; Phil 1.29 (though most mss read "granted to *you*," not so supportive of Chrysostom's point).

¹⁰ 1 Sam 2.2. This is as much as Chrysostom takes of Hannah's prayer (1 Sam 2.1-10, a significant backdrop, of course, to the Lukan Magnificat) after three homilies on it. His beau ideal Paul is proving a richer source for his teaching than his putative heroine.

¹¹ 1 Cor 4.5. Just as occasion was taken of a brief sentiment of Hannah's for a disquisition on prayer, now a similar essay is developed on divine providence. The biblical text itself is not providing sufficient material, obviously, and despite the length of this further essay the homily is relatively brief.

[12] Chrysostom is a great rationalizer; normally the last to defend riches for riches sake and uphold deprivation of the poor, he can when pressed make a case for poverty, as he also does in commenting on Ps 4, where he declares poverty (for which he had no economic solution) to be "the mother of wisdom." Any port in a storm has been the axiom of many a preacher. In both instances, however, one wonders if any poor people present would find the argument anything but specious.

[13] We have strayed far from the topic of divine providence, and even further from Hannah and her prayer prompting it. The preacher has warmed to a favorite theme (enlivening perhaps his most powerful psalm commentary, on Ps 49), the vanity of the idle rich, especially in death.

[14] Prov 9.9.

[15] The preacher seems to have forgotten what was the principal theme of this homily, and in fact of the series of which it is the conclusion. Hannah has gone, though there is just the suggestion of the topic of divine providence from which he strayed to dwell upon the limitations of the situation of the rich. There is certainly no sign of his being tempted to prolong the homily or the series; he perhaps wondered if he had misjudged the potentiality of the Former Prophets for his ministry, especially as his listeners voted against them with their feet. The races were not wholly to blame.

General Index

Index of Biblical Citations

Breinigsville, PA USA
03 June 2010
239161BV00001B/9/A